Rose Haven Farm

The Life of Mary Cranston Green
A Wise and Wonderful Woman 1867—1965

Katherine R. Inman

Mayhaven Publishing, Inc
P O Box 557
Mahomet, IL 61853
USA

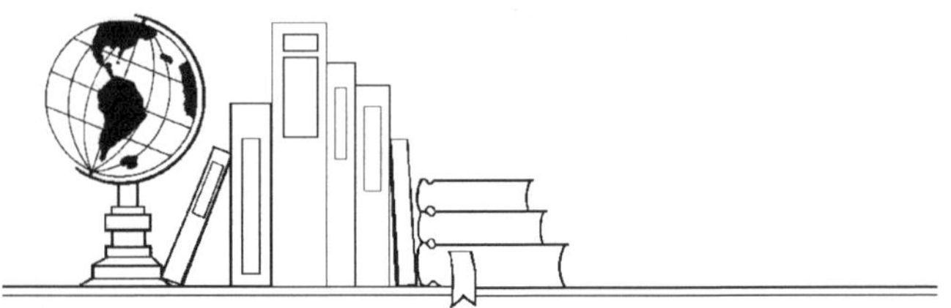

Cover Design: Doris Replogle Wenzel
Library of Congress Control Number: 2010926449
First Edition—First Printing 2010
ISBN 13: 9781932278-57-6
ISBN 10: 1932278-57-5

At right: Mary Cranston Green

Acknowledgements

There are so many people to thank! Thanks to Debbie, Cathy, Roger, and Steve for proof reading and fact checking. My computer expert sons, Richard and Roger have helped immeasurably with putting the parts together and searching information for historic accuracy. My friend and aunt, Lois Green, sent me the memories of her husband Vivian Green. Many of my cousins have contributed memories of interesting incidents, and gathered newspaper articles, genealogies, obituaries and writings of their parents, our grandmother, and great grandparents. I thank Roberta Green, Mary Margaret Woods and Betty Wood. Even the cousins of my cousins, who loved their vacations on the Rose Haven Farm, have shared fondest memories. I thank Don and Harold Colbert, too, and Delores Green, widow of the third generation owner of Rose Haven Farm, for providing much of the information of the Cousin's Reunion, the Centennial Celebration, and the growth of the farm. For the last chapters, she and Kevin and Sue Green, fourth generation owners, gave me updates and a wonderful tour of today's Rose Haven Farm in May of 2008, and updates until the time of this writing.

The poems of my grandmother were gathered by my aunt Ruth Green Gordon, who also wrote the story "Stuck in the Mud." I believe Kevin or Dolores gave me my grandmother's published story of "The Pond" and the copy of the *History of Oakwood.* I do appreciate having them. These are in the appendix. I also want to give appreciation to the University of Illinois for contributing so much to each of the five generations of this family.

I used my treasured memories of my grandmother and my many vacations on the Rose Haven Farm, and my mother Alta Green Ropiequet's memories, too. I filled in all the cracks with my imagination. All the facts I can verify, and all the memories in writing were given to me directly.

Most of all, I thank my God who has inspired me to make my wonderful grandmother's story, and that of the family farm, available for her progeny and for everyone who can benefit from her faith, wisdom, courage, ingenuity and insistence on education in turning tragedy and hardships into triumph, love and encouragement for many, many people.

Table of Contents

Illustrations:

Left: Mary Cranston Green, on whose life much of this memoir is based, with granddaughter Edith (sitting), and eldest daughter Alta - 1936.

An original watercolor of Rose Haven Farm
by Katherine "Kit" (Green) Inman. Date unknown.

Prologue

Picture rose bushes lining a country dirt road, a driveway on both sides, and a garden, bright with color. This was Rose Haven Farm in the 1890's, owned and developed by my grandparents Lincoln H. and Mary Cranston Green. This is their story, and especially Mary's, who lived to be ninety-eight, and the story of the farm, all of which influenced and inspired five generations of educated, honorable people. The University of Illinois has a place in this story, too.

Both Lincoln and Mary were children of pioneers who came in covered wagons to settle in Illinois. Their families believed in education, faith, and hard work. They overcame hardships, tragedies, and daunting challenges with persistence, ingenuity, and wisdom, always strong in faith. Mary began as a teacher just after finishing eighth grade, afterward attending three colleges. Lincoln chose divinity school, but ended up a farmer. They both had many talents, hobbies, and activities to enrich their lives. The Rose Haven Farm became a learning tool, provided joy, and was character builder for their children, their children's children, and is still a magnet for the Green generations.

Though the story focuses on Lincoln and Mary, the farm, too, had a life and personality of its own. I started with genealogy, written memories, newspaper records, anecdotes shared by family letters, telephone conversations, my own memories, and filled in the gaps with my imagination. Mary Cranston Green was a wise and wonderful woman whose memory still inspires her progeny, and the farm she and Lincoln started is still alive and thriving today.

Part I

Mary Esther Cranston

Home from College

In June 1887, as Mary Esther Cranston stepped down from the stool by the train steps, she hung the large valise over her shoulder and turned to her brother, Leslie Cranston, struggling down the steps with two large suitcases saying, "I don't see them. They must be late."

"They'll be here. Let's go into the station."

Before they could reach the door, their parents, Julius and Artemissa Cranston, came out smiling. "Here, Leslie, let me help with those," Julius said grasping a suitcase in one hand and Leslie's hand in the other. "Congratulations, Mr. Attorney. You passed the bar exam on the first try. We're so proud of you!"

Artemissa gave her daughter a hug. "You've been away a long time. We really missed you at Christmas."

Mary Esther answered, "I know. I missed you, too. But Cousin Anne and Uncle John Cranston invited me to spend Christmas with them. It was wonderful. They welcomed me as if we'd known each other all our lives. She wanted to know every little thing about you and our family. It was wonderful having Anna as a roommate. She helped me get started."

Artemissa hugged her daughter, again. "You'll have to tell us all about them. You're glowing, Mary Esther. Antioch College must have been good for you."

Mary's blue eyes were shining, and her dark blond hair, loosely gathered in a bun on top, was a soft frame for her oval face, and emphasized her height, slightly taller than most women. "Mother, Papa, thank you for sending me. I love learning, and I had the best professors.

"It seems you both did well at Antioch," Julius said, "But it's good to have you home."

"Papa," Leslie said hesitantly, "I'm going to go back to Ohio in July. Mr. Stevenson, a well-thought-of attorney in Yellow Springs, has asked me to join him in his law practice. I admire him, and appreciate a chance to work with an experienced, honorable attorney."

"That sounds like a wise decision. Gibson City doesn't offer much for a law practice. It's time for you to start your career, but we'll miss you." Julius led the way to their buggy and they loaded the suitcases in silence.

Artemissa commented as they took their places in the buggy, "We have news for you, but we'll wait until we get home. You must be tired, coming all the way from Ohio."

As they pulled into the driveway of the white frame house several miles northeast of Gibson City, Mary Esther saw her grandmother Roxanne Atwood, waiting, holding brother Artie—three, by the hand. Clara Jeanette—twenty-four, Lucy—nineteen, Stephen—eighteen, and Grace—nine, ran out to greet them. Mary Esther missed Phoebe, her little blind sister, who would have been seven, but had died just a year earlier, of tuberculosis.

Mary Esther forgot how tired she was as she greeted her family. When Leslie and his father returned from taking care of the horses, the greetings were repeated, and then they sat down at the long table full of their favorite foods. There was much to thank the Lord for, but after the grace, Mary Esther impatiently asked, "What is the news you couldn't tell me at the station?"

Everybody looked at Clara Jeanette, who blushed as she said, "I'm going to be married in just three weeks, and, Mary, you're back just in time to be my maid of honor."

"Who's the lucky man? Is it that tall farmer, Lincoln Green? Or—"

Clara interrupted Mary. "Not anyone you know. It's Stephen Waggoner. He came here to gather and prepare a wagon train to Kansas. He's a wagon master like the one with whom Father was going to take us to Kansas in 1876. He's been there, and you should hear him describe the wide, beautiful skies with dramatic sunsets, and the fields of golden grain waving in the wind. He says he's found the perfect place for a homestead, near a little stream with some trees. There aren't many trees in Kansas, but there are some. And Stephen's so strong and handsome with his dark hair and beard. When he first came to the church youth group, the beard was long and shaggy, but now it's neatly trimmed." Clara stopped for a breath.

Julius added, "He's a fine Christian man, with an education, too. And he's a good leader, well organized, in control, but gentle, too. The only problem is that he's going to take Clara away to Kansas."

Mary Esther asked, "Won't you miss teaching? You've really enjoyed your time at Dixon School. That makes three of us who've taught school there: Leslie, me, and you. It will be hard for them to find a new teacher. They couldn't find a teacher for Dixon School, and that's why they asked me to teach right after I finished eighth grade there. Simon Barnes tutored Alice and me in higher learning in our seventh and eighth grades, and kept on during the two years I was teaching. He was a good teacher; good enough to prepare me for college."

"I remember those years. You had to work long, hard hours to keep ahead of your upper grades. I do enjoy teaching, but maybe there will be enough settlers to have a school there." Mary detected a tiny bit of longing in Clara Jeanette's voice.

"Leslie joked, "Maybe you could teach the Indians."

"Why not?" Clara answered. "Mary, just wait until you meet Stephen. Tomorrow we'll talk about the wedding plans, and Sunday we'll invite Stephen for dinner."

Stephen was charming, and a gentleman. When he and Clara joined Leslie, Mary, and Lucy in the Brethren youth group Sunday evening, he was completely at ease with the familiar friends of Gibson City even though Clara said he had been there only two months.

Mary Esther was surprised to see Lincoln Green there, too. He must be at least twenty-four, she thought.

Leslie greeted him warmly, and asked, "Lincoln, I hear you've bought your own farm next to your father's?"

Lincoln laughed. "It's only 50 acres, just a start. I still help my father, too. I hear you passed your law exam. Congratulations."

Leslie laughed, too. "Thanks. I'll know better when I start practicing. I'm going back to Yellow Springs to join a law firm."

Lincoln turned to Mary Esther to comment, "And how about you? Not many women go to college. I think they should get higher education if they can. My mother found her college courses helped her teach us at home until Gibson City built their schools."

"Yes, and very well, I've heard." Mary added, "Many people think it's completely unnecessary for women to have higher education. I love to learn. During Leslie's last year at Antioch, Father persuaded me to go, too. My cousin Anna Cranston, a senior there, was my roommate. She made it easy for me to get good classes and professors. I had a wonderful year. Her parents even invited me to spend Christmas vacation with them."

"I like to learn, too." Lincoln responded. "As soon as my father can manage his farm without me, I intend to go to Adrian College. I still read a lot."

Stephen came over to ask Lincoln, "We're going to be homesteading in Kansas. Can you give me some advice on building our house? I hear you had a lean-to before you built yours."

As they talked, Mary Esther joined a group of her high school classmates who kept her busy answering questions about college.

When the young people settled into their chairs, Mary discovered why Lincoln Green was with the younger people. He was the speaker. Mary listened as he urged the young people to plan their lives, and work toward their plans, but he also said that when their interests and circumstances changed, they should be flexible, and change their plans, always working toward fulfilling them. But then, he added, for a happy and successful life, it is important to make sure your plans are compatible with God's plans for your life. Mary considered her plans. They were most uncertain. All she knew was that she wanted to learn more and more.

Clara's wedding plans filled the days until July 3, 1887. It would be a simple wedding in the roomy home of her grandmother Atwood, and her wedding dress had to be a practical gown she could use as a pioneer in Kansas. She chose navy blue poplin with a white lace collar. It seemed to match her eyes and accent her blond hair. Artemissa gave her a cameo pin she had received from *her* grandmother in Vermont, saying, "You are as beautiful as the lady carved in the cameo." Clara blushed, and hugged her mother. Mary Esther also chose blue, but like an October sky. With the wedding dress finished, the two challenges were to plan the guest list and the reception, but more importantly, to gather the limited essentials to outfit the wagon and prepare to establish a home. Stephen was a big help, as he had been guide and wagon master for several wagon trains. Artemissa consulted with Stephen to gather the trousseau, making sure each garment was suited to the hot summers and cold, windy prairie winters.

No sooner had they celebrated the wedding and bid God speed to Mr. and Mrs. Stephen Waggoner, than they had to concentrate on Leslie's departure to Yellow Springs. He had kept his secret until Clara Jeanette was properly loved, honored, and blessed as the wagon disappeared from their sight. He announced at dinner that night, "Mama, Papa, there's a woman in Yellow Springs whom, as soon as I get settled in a law practice and have a little money, I'm going to ask to marry me. Her name is Lillian Hope Maury. I met her at the Methodist Church in Yellow Springs, in the college class. She's beautiful, with dark hair and sparkling eyes, and a wonderful smile. Mary knows her, too, but I made her promise not to tell you about her. I met her parents. Her father is a doctor, and her mother teaches Sunday School. I'll bring her here to meet you when I can. You'll love her."

The hurrying began again. In a week, they drove Leslie back to the train station with a trunk of his belongings. It seemed so final to Mary Esther. She and Leslie had grown even closer in college. Now

Clara Jeanette, and Leslie, were gone miles and miles away to new lives, and here she was, twenty, and no idea what she would do with her life. She had been popular enough at Antioch. She met lots of intelligent and gentlemanly men, and several of them had been interested in her, but they all seemed so dedicated to their careers and earning money. They didn't even notice the beauty of a sunset, or tree, or flower. They didn't seem to enjoy reading anything but their textbooks. There wasn't a spark between any of them and her. Maybe she could teach again. People had said she was a good teacher—but not like Clara Jeanette. Clara was so excited about each student who did well, and worried about those that didn't. Maybe she could be a good teacher, too. Mary might have inherited the talent from her mother. She had taught a few years before she married Mary's father. But Mary was more interested in plants and flowers, the "Lilies of the field." They were so intricately and individually beautiful, each in its own way, from the tiny grass flowers to the giant oaks.

Undecided

The next day, Mary Esther walked over to her grandfather Cranston's house. After greetings, she said, "I need something to do. I came to look for a good book."

"Come on in to the library. I think you need something more than a book." Julius Cranston Sr.'s blue eyes, shaded by thick white brows matching his white hair and beard, met Mary Esther's troubled look. He could sense her discontent. "I can tell, Mary, you're at a crossroads, and want someone to listen, and let you untangle the questions."

"Somehow I knew you'd understand. Here I am, Grandpapa, twenty years old, and I don't know which way to go. Aunt Melissa knew—she wanted to be a doctor, and she did it. Clara Jeanette loved being a teacher, and she will be happy, even in Kansas, with Stephen. I should apply for Clara Jeanette's teaching position."

"You were a good teacher, even right out of eighth grade. I remember hours of preparation and studying higher learning, even as you taught." Julius Cranston studied Mary's eyes as she gazed through him into the past.

"Those two years were pleasant. I was learning so much from

teaching as well as the tutoring Simon was giving me. It was all right, and the next years of teaching, too, but not for a career."

Julius studied Mary's face for a few moments, and then asked, "What about your college? Did you find any learning there that would give you inspiration for a career?"

Mary Esther's eyes lit up. "Maybe. Professor Benderson even took us on Botany field trips. It was fascinating. I know how to identify almost any plant, and how to take care of them. But identifying flowers isn't a career. We looked through a telescope at the stars in Professor Wells' Astronomy class, and Professor Tufts even made mathematics interesting—especially geometry—but not interesting enough to spend my life measuring triangles and rectangles. And I joined the Athenaeum Literary Society. We shared our writings, and they all said my poems were very good. Should I join the 'Poor Poet's Society?' "

Again, Mary's blue eyes focused far away as she added, "I probably could have married Robert, one of the men I met at Antioch College, but I couldn't see myself locked into being a housewife for a man wanting only a career and money. There's so much wonder and beauty in the world, so much more to learn and explore. I'd love to be a perpetual student, but that's no career, and it wouldn't help anyone else, either. You and your father risked everything to help escaping slaves in Ohio. What did they call it?"

"The Underground Railroad. It was an exciting time. We didn't believe any man should be a slave, especially here in America where freedom is what our ancestors fought for." Julius Cranston, Sr., too, seemed lost in memories for a while.

"Grandfather, we all admire you for your courage and ideals. Is there a cause today that would be worth risking my life for? But I need to find a way to support myself, too. I don't want to be a burden on my father forever. I probably should accept the teaching job in Dixon School. They've asked me. But I don't want to be an old maid school teacher."

"That is a tangle. Let's see. We can take away the doctor, but a teacher doesn't have to be one forever, and not an old maid. Maybe being a student doesn't need to be perpetual, and maybe marriage isn't impossible if the right man should come along. Mary, maybe it's not time to make a final choice. Sometimes God says, 'Wait.'"

"But Mama doesn't need much help and what would I do while I'm waiting? My hands don't like to be still. I could plant a lovely garden, I guess. I should, she reiterated, replace Clara Jeanette teaching in Dixon School. I guess I will, but I'd rather teach Botany. Maybe I can sneak in a few lessons." Mary sighed.

"Mary, I think I know exactly what you need right now, but I'll have to look into it. You help Artemissa with dinner while I go talk to someone. I'll be back by the time dinner is ready." Julius grinned and patted her shoulder, and left the library.

Mary and her grandmother worked and talked, and before long dinner was ready and the table set. Her grandfather walked in just in time. "As soon as we finish dinner, Mary, I'm going to take you to see Mr. Davis." That was all he would say about it.

Mr. Davis was waiting on a customer when Mary Esther and her grandfather entered his general store. He was of medium height, lean, with rough hands. Mary and Julius waited patiently while he climbed onto a stool and fetched a clothesbasket from a high shelf, totaled the bill for the widow Smithson, and loaded the groceries in a basket. He carried it out to her buggy and returned with big smile lighting up his hazel eyes. There was a touch of grey in his beard, but none in his dark wavy hair. He shook Julius hand and turned to Mary. "Julius here has told me you've finished a couple of courses in Botany at that college in Ohio. Would you happen to be open to helping me out a little here in the store this summer? I'm planning to open a section to sell plants and seeds, and in addition to farming supplies, provide some special tools for flower and vegetable gardens. The farm supplies I've been handling all along, but I don't know much about home gardens, or flowers, or house plants. I never had time to plant anything myself."

Mary looked quickly at her grandfather and laughed. "Mr. Davis, I would be pleased to help you plan a garden section. I can see Grandfather Cranston has been telling tales about me. Studying Botany was exciting. When you have time, we can talk about exactly what you have in mind." Mary glanced at the waiting customers.

"If it's all right with you, Mary, I'll come over tonight after I close the store."

Mary nodded, and Mr. Davis smiled as he turned to his customers.

Mr. Davis knocked on the Atwood door about 8 p.m. Mary was waiting, light hearted, thinking of the garden section. She couldn't think of anything she'd rather do than plan and work with flowers and plants the entire summer—but she didn't want to be a clerk. Mr. Davis greeted the family and started talking enthusiastically, "Mary, you are just what I needed. I've had this idea for a couple of years, but I don't know enough to make it work. People around here have been working hard just to get their farms and homes going, but now it's time for them to have a little beauty in their lives. Flowers give a lift to the heart, a rainbow of promise."

"Mr. Davis, these farmers' wives have been saving seeds from year to year to have some flowers in their gardens. Both Grandmother Atwood and Grandmother Cranston had flowers in their gardens: larkspur, coreopsis, morning glories on the fences, hollyhocks—Clara Jeanette and I used to make dolls of them, blossoms for dresses and buds for heads—such fun. I understand the desire to branch out a little more." Mary waited a moment, and asked, "What is your dream?"

"Beautiful flowers in every garden, all kinds, and flowering plants in the homes in winter." Mr. Davis laughed. "But that's a dream, and I don't have any idea how or where to start. What kind of flowers will flourish in this climate? Which ones are hardy and easy to grow, and are still a little exotic, and not too expensive? I know about seeds and some bulbs, and some nurseries grow plants and bushes to sell, but that would take years and lots of experience. And what about house plants? I need someone who knows about these things. Your grandfather tells me you have studied Botany this past year at Antioch College, and you would be able to help me."

"That's a beautiful dream, Mr. Davis, and I'd be honored to help you plan and begin. I have decided to accept the teaching position at Dixon School, but I have the rest of this summer before that starts. Do you have space in your store for displays? We could make a little garden corner to start with, if there is space by a window, and perhaps an area outside for a garden display and a place to hold flowering shrubs to be planted in the fall. It's too late now to start many of the plants, but fall is a good time for some. It's ambitious, but perhaps you would like to build a little greenhouse to grow seedlings and house plants. There's a fine nursery in Champaign-Urbana where you could find the initial plants and surprise Gibson City with a beautiful selection from the very start."

"Your grandfather was right. I can hardly wait to begin. When can you start, Mary?"

"I can start right away. Tomorrow morning," Mary answered as they walked toward the chairs in the corner to make plans.

Mary Esther walked to Mr. Davis' store early the next morning, with two of her grandmother's nursery catalogs in her knitting bag and her mind full of ideas. It was midsummer, but there were a few plants that could survive the heat, and many more for fall planting. Mr. Davis was already there, looking for the best space near the front window. Mary had found the answer to her uncertainty. This was exactly what she wanted to do, and she knew she could do it well and still be a good teacher. In two weeks, the nursery section inside the front window was ready for stocking, and Mr. Davis and Mary left the store in the hands of Emmet Green, his current clerk, and drove to the nursery to purchase the initial stock, colorful, but practical, and not too expensive. They also bought fall flowering shrubs, and only one of a Crepe Myrtle tree's rooted twig as she knew they were not usually hardy enough for East Central Illinois winters.

On the first Saturday in August, the display was ready, and the plants all priced. Mary had made a sign, "FLOWERS: Brighten Your Life." There was a mixed response. Some farmers went past with hardly a glance, absorbed with needed purchases, but most of the women stopped to look carefully, and note the prices. Many of them came back after they had gathered their listed goods, and bought at least one plant. Her grandfather came by to admire the display and buy some plants for his wife, and Mary's father stopped by to express his approval.

About 5 p.m., Lincoln Green came into the store to talk to his brother Emmet, and give him a ride home on his horse. He glanced at the flowers, and then stopped to talk to Mary. She watched him look from one bright flower to another, his big hands moving gently, as if ready to caress, above the display of geraniums, cleomes, larkspur, a large pot with hostas, zinnias, caryopsis and more.

"They're lovely, Mary, and such a good idea. I remember my mother saving seeds in Ohio to bring to Illinois, flower as well as vegetable. She doesn't have as many flowers any more. She needs something that blooms every year without giving her any hard work. Maybe you have something beautiful that will bloom every year."

"Chrysanthemums bloom well into the fall, and are perennials. They come in several colors and often bloom until frost. If you wanted something really excitedly beautiful, we brought one special bush, or tree, that might be exactly what your want. It's a crepe myrtle. But maybe not. It will take a year or two to be in full flower, though there should be a few blossoms next August. The blossoms are large clusters of flowers in a lovely dark pink, as big as your hand, Lincoln, and they bloom in late summer when not much else is blooming. It was a foolish plant to buy, I guess, but it is so beautiful when it's in full bloom. The chrysanthemums, however, are a better buy for this year."

"You said a tree? How big does it grow?" Lincoln asked.

"I saw one in Yellow Springs as high as the house. It starts out looking like a bush, gets pretty big, and then the trunk develops, and it becomes a tree. It takes eight or more years to look more like a tree than a bush, but it's pretty both ways. I've seen clusters of blossoms ten inches long, and about eight inches thick."

"I'll buy it for my mother, but I'll take one of these chrysanthemums to give color until the crepe myrtle blooms. I'm impressed with how much you and Mr. Davis have accomplished. It's good to have this beauty available here."

Lincoln waited, watching intently while Mary collected and packaged the plants. Then, a bit hesitant, asked, "Mary, would you be free Sunday after church to take a buggy ride with me, maybe find a place for a picnic?"

Surprised, Mary looked up, meeting his deep blue eyes and gentle smile, she said softly, "I would be delighted, Lincoln." Laughing, she added, "I'd be glad to bring a picnic."

"Not this time. I have a plan. Maybe next time, Mary." Mary felt a little thrill at the music in his voice as he said her name, and at the hint of a next time.

A miniature blueprinting of flower by Mary C. Green.
Date unknown.

Secret Places

Lincoln was talking to the Reverend Franklin when Mary came out of church with her family. He stepped aside to let the Cranstons shake hands with the minister, then led Mary to a horse and buggy.

"Where are we going to picnic, Lincoln?" Mary asked.

"I want to surprise you. You'll like it." Lincoln answered. "It's a perfect August day, warm but with a gentle breeze. I discovered this place one day when I was chasing a deer. Did you ever hear my father's story of hunting the big deer?" Lincoln laughed, and spoke in a deepened drawl, "A big, big deer was ruining his corn, tearing down the stalks and eating the ears, and breaking down a fence into the wheat field, trampling the grain as he fed. And then, one early morning he broke down the fence to the chicken yard, knocked the lid off the bucket of seed feed, and ate it all. Father was raging. In November, he told Mother, 'The crops are in, the cattle fed and in the stalls. I'm going to shoot that big deer, and I'll not come home until I get him." Father went to the woods hunting for the tracks of the big deer. He found lots of tracks of little deer, but it took him until noon to find the big tracks. He followed them, and in an hour he saw the deer grazing in another farmer's field, but as he approached, the deer bounded away. He followed the tracks, and came close a number of times, but the deer always stopped feeding and raced off. Father was persistent, but it was near the end of the second day when he saw the deer feeding in a cornfield with shocks of corn. He hid behind one shock after another, and finally got close enough to shoot without the deer seeing him. He was a good shot, and killed the deer. But there he was miles and miles from home, and there was no way he could carry the big deer with those huge antlers. He walked to a farm house in the distance, knocked on the door, and asked the farmer if he would be kind enough to help him get the deer home. The farmer went to look at the deer, and said, 'I'll help you, but let's get some supper first.'"

"Your father must have been very, very hungry by then," Mary commented.

"Probably," Lincoln agreed, "but he was so intent on getting that deer, he did not think of anything else. The farmer's wife had a fine supper ready, and in the late November evening they used leverage to load the deer into the farmer's wagon. Then they started out toward Father's farm near Zenia, Ohio. It was twenty miles away! It was almost dawn when the wagon rolled into the barnyard. Father called out, waking Mother, "Augusta, I got him. Come and see." They invited the farmer to have breakfast, and then the two of them skinned the deer, hung the skin up to dry, and butchered the big deer. There was a lot of meat. Father gave the farmer a quarter for his kindness in bringing my father and the deer home. Our family had dried and smoked venison all winter."

"How long did you track the deer the time you found the picnic place?" Mary asked. "And did you shoot him?"

"It must have been four or five hours, but I did get him. Father taught me to shoot. It was just an average size, but the venison was good." Lincoln turned the horses from the road into a faint set of wagon tracks. "We're almost there." Ahead was a grove of trees. Lincoln stopped the buggy under a shady tree, and helped Mary down. After pegging the horse to let him graze, he picked up a blanket and a large basket. "It's just a little way down this path."

Mary heard the trickling water before they reached the stream. There was a little waterfall, and rapids foaming over rocks. Beside the stream was a meadow filled with daisies and wild purple flocks, with one big rock not far from the stream. "Oh, Lincoln, it's lovely."

Lincoln spread the blanket near the rock, and the cloth cover from the basket on the rock, and spread out the food before them. He had fried chicken, boiled eggs, raw carrots, celery sticks, some green broccoli, two pieces of chocolate cake, and two bright red apples. He took two glasses from the basket, and dipped water from the stream. "Your majesty, enjoy your repast."

Mary made a mock curtsy and sat down near the rock, and as Lincoln joined her she said, "This is a feast fit for a queen. Are you a cook, too, or did your mother join in the conspiracy? It does look delicious."

"I'll confess. I asked Mother to fry a couple of extra pieces of chicken last night, and helped myself to two pieces of the cake she baked for dinner today. The rest I fixed. I can cook a little, Mary."

After Mary had enjoyed a chicken thigh, Lincoln handed her a napkin, and said, "I was surprised to see you working at Mr. Davis' store, and to find that new flower section."

"It surprised me as much as it did you. I was telling Grandfather Cranston that I just didn't know what I wanted to do with my life. He's a great listener. Actually, it was your talk to the youth group last month that started me thinking. All I really wanted to do was to learn, and maybe work with plants and flowers. After I mentioned the plants, his eyes lit up, and he said there was someone he wanted to talk to. He wouldn't say another word. He took me to see Mr. Davis at his store. Mr. Davis shared his desire to set up a flower department, but also that he needed someone who knew more about flowers. It was just what I'd like to do. He asked if he could come after his store closed that evening to make plans with me. He said he had been wanting to set up a section of his store to sell plants and flowers, because people need a little beauty in their lives after the hard work of homesteading. But, he said, he didn't know anything about flowers and flowering plants. He knew I had studied botany at Antioch College and asked me if I would be willing to help him develop a floral corner. Lincoln, I couldn't think of anything I'd rather do, right now. Not for very long, but I'd like to help him spread beauty in East Bend Township." Mary's blue eyes were shining. "I've agreed to teach in Dixon School this year, since Clara Jeanette is gone."

"It's a wonderful thing to do. When we came here from Ohio, Mother brought flower seeds as well as vegetables, and we had pretty flowers, but after Herbert and John left, Mother let the flowers go. There was too much farm work. I've been trying to encourage her to bring back the flowers." Lincoln looked at the meadow of flowers. "They're pretty, aren't they? Why don't we pick a bouquet when we leave?"

"I'd like that, but be sure to take your mother one, and leave enough to reseed for next year. I'm curious, Lincoln. Why did you stay here instead of going off to college or to homestead?"

"Father needed help with the farm. We had planted most of the 160 acres to help pay off the loan, and with my older brothers gone, it was just too much for one man to farm. Wilbert and I were young and still in school, and Emmet was still a toddler. I sort of grew up being a partner with Father. I've bought a little farm near our homestead land. I have a dream of studying for the ministry, but Father still needs me"

Mary Esther was impressed with his consideration for his parents. "I heard you tell that to Leslie. It's a noble profession. My father went to Seminary in Mechanicsburg, Ohio, but he chose farming instead of preaching. My Aunt Melissa is a minister in Kansas."

Lincoln was silent for a few moments. "I think I always was interested in the Bible. The night before we set out for Illinois, I remember Father reading the 139th Psalm. I asked him to reread the part about how it was impossible to get away from the presence of God—verses 7 to 10. It gave me such peace to know God would be with us all along the way and in Illinois, too. And In heaven, and even in hell. And He has been with us. It would be an honor to serve such a God."

Mary said, half to herself, "My father never did serve as a minister in a church, but he did minister to our family and to friends and neighbors in need. I remember in the early days there were only circuit preachers every three months or so. When they came to the area, men rode to all the farms to tell people the preacher was here, and they would come to Father's farm with all their children and baskets of food. They'd stay all day for preaching—morning and afternoon, funerals and weddings—and fellowship. Other Sundays, some would come anyway, and sometimes my father would give a little talk. He helped a lot of people."

"Our family usually went to your father's home on Sundays, and when no minister was there, your father led a beautiful service."

After a few moments of enjoying the food, Lincoln asked, "Don't I remember a baby called Mary Esther?"

"I was just a year old when we moved from here. We lived in Ford County until I was nine. I started school in Clempson School—a little country school. There were big switches on the wall to keep the boys in order. The teacher used them, too. We had desks for two, and my teacher, Mr. Jackson, a stern, tall man, made George Metcalf, mischievous and always in trouble, sit with me"

"Then did he behave?" Lincoln asked.

"He teased the girls during recess, and fought with the boys. In class, Mr. Jackson often hit him on the head." Mary paused a moment, then added, "He died that spring of brain fever. I wondered if that was caused by the hits on his head."

"It would make you wonder, but probably not," Lincoln commented, and changed to a more pleasant subject. "We played games during recess, catch, prisoner's base, tag—"Lincoln reached over and touched Mary on the shoulder, saying, "You're it."

Mary laughed, saying, "We played those, too, and in the lower grades, "Drop the Handkerchief. I was glad when they transferred me, in second grade, to a bigger school a mile north—Union School. There we played Dare Base, and the boys played baseball. I was in third grade, nine years old, when we came back to Gibson City. Then I attended the Dixon School with your family.

"It was in 1876. Father sold his land in Ford County, and the 120 acres he had purchased here in 1857. He had intended to homestead in Kansas, but when Grandfather Atwood died, Father decided to stay with his mother-in-law and farm their land. I'm glad he did. I don't think Kansas has any schools and certainly no colleges. Clara Jeanette was excited about being a pioneer there with Stephen, but I'd rather be in Illinois. When we left here to go to Ford County, it was just East Bend Township, but when we came back, it had grown, moved a few miles north, and was already Gibson City." Mary Esther turned to Lincoln to ask, "Were you born here in East Bend Township?"

"I was born in Zenia, Ohio. We came here by covered wagon when I was six. It was an exciting journey. There was a blizzard, and three rivers to ford. One wagon got stuck in the middle of the Wabash River. It was deep, almost over the wheels. During the blizzard, my mother taught us classes in the wagon. The first night the cattle wandered away, Mr. Henderson's sheep dog helped find them and herd them back. Did you travel by covered wagon to Ford County?"

"Yes, but I don't remember it. But we did come back here in one, planning to go on to Kansas. I read most of the way. My father had just given me a book of Chinese adventure tales."

Mary looked away. She had not enjoyed the trip. "My father came here by covered wagon from Champaign County, Ohio, where he was born. My grandfather Atwood came from Ohio to Wolford, Illinois, in 1854 and moved to East Bend County ten years later. He and Grandmother Roxanne were both born and married in Stowe, Vermont."

Lincoln waited for her attention. "Our parents did a lot of moving to new farms, didn't they? My grandfather came to America from England and settled in Pennsylvania, then moved to Ohio. He's still there, with several of my aunts and uncles. My father decided to come here to homestead. The Homestead Act of 1862 offered free land to anyone who would stake it out, build some kind of home in six months. After five years the land was theirs. Father found a great piece of land, 160 acres, with a stream and trees. But our first attempt to build a house was discouraging."

Mary Esther didn't remember her parents building a house. There was one in Ford County they purchased, and the house in East

Bend had been built before she was born. "Tell me, how do you go about building a house?"

"The first one we tried to build was a lean-to. That's a three-sided house of logs with a crude roof of logs and sod. Father and my two older brothers cut some trees from the woods on our lot, some 20 feet long and some 12-feet long, and a lot of pieces about ten inches long. Then they chopped notches in all and built walls by putting the shorter pieces between the long ones, and the little pieces on the other end of the shorter pieces. In about two weeks, it was ready for the roof. Then it started raining, and raining. They had to quit work, and Sunday we drove into the little group of houses near Mr. Davis' store. We gathered at your grandfather's house for church, It had been raining for several days, and when we got back, the ground was flooded by our stream, and the logs, most of them, floated downstream. It was March, and cold, but father and my brothers waded into the stream to retrieve the logs. They found most of them. But we had learned a lesson. Don't build on a flood plain"

"Did you rebuild on higher ground? And did you have a house within the six months?" Mary Esther could sense the discouragement they must have felt.

"Yes and no. Mother insisted that we had to get the crops in before we tried to build again. We still slept in the wagons. The next Sunday, father was talking to your grandfather about the house, and Mr. Cranston suggested that he build a real house. He could take logs to the mill to make boards, and buy supplies he couldn't make himself. He said he would be glad to recommend Father for a loan. While you have two husky sons to help you build, that's the time to build a real house."

Lincoln remembered the hard work they all did. "Mr. Cranston helped us with the plans, lending his. You have a wonderful grandfather, Mary. After the crops were planted, we all worked night and day cutting logs. Mother even helped with the cross blade saw. They cleared one wagon to haul the logs to the mill every week, and brought back cut lumber and needed supplies. Melissa, Victoria and I helped, too. We watched Emma and Wilbert, but we also stacked the smaller branches Melissa cut with a saw, gathered even smaller ones for kindling and then, I had an idea. I decided that we could use the smaller, straight branches to make a chicken house. Victoria and I had been taking care of the crate of chickens on the entire trip, and still brought water and feed to them. Melissa and Victoria helped, and we did build a chicken house. My brothers had to help with the roof, and in the few unstructured moments, my brothers put the rescued logs together to build a lean-to for the horses and cattle. After father bought a wheelbarrow, Victoria and I gathered rocks from the stream for a foundation for the house. Every one worked really hard. Even Emma tried to bring wood. Wilbert was too little, but he was well behaved.

"Lincoln, did you finish in six months?"

"No, but by September we had the kitchen done, and moved into that. It was large, and much better than the wagons, and we had bought a cook stove that made it much warmer." Lincoln proudly added, "We did have it all finished by early November, and that was when Mother started the home school for us and our neighbors."

"Could your mother teach even high school boys?" Mary asked.

"Herbert and John went to work, Herbert for Mr. Davis, and John for the widow Wellington. She owned the little hotel. They wanted to help pay off the debt. But the second year, Herbert went back to Ohio to study law and get married, and John kept working in the hotel and took lessons from Mrs. Wellington. He went to

Illinois College the third year."

"It's remarkable, Lincoln, how your family worked together. I've seen your home—it's large, and very attractive."

"We didn't want to live in wagons any longer than necessary, and the lean-to didn't look much better. Mary, it's exciting to build things. And we were a big family and needed a big house."

"I know. We need a big house, too. Grandmother Atwood's house is a little small, but with Leslie and Clara Jeanette gone, we have plenty of room. I miss them, though."

Mary had grown very close to Leslie even with their age difference while they were at Antioch College.

"Mary, how about next Sunday? Will you join me for another picnic?" Lincoln started gathering the remnants into the basket. Mary helped.

"I've really enjoyed this, but next week, let me show you *my* secret place, and I'll bring the lunch. Now, let's gather our bouquets." Mary and Lincoln each gathered a handful of flowers, and started to lay them in the picnic basket. Mary suggested, "Let's get a little water in these glasses, wet napkins to wrap the stems, and keep them fresher until we get home." Then, a bit reluctantly, they picked up the picnic basket of flowers, followed the little path to the buggy, and shared stories of their lives on the way back.

The flower section was busy the next week, and on Friday, again Mr. Davis and Mary went to the Champaign County nursery to replenish supplies and expand the selection. Mary suggested they plant pots of bulbs for house plants during the winter, and sell selections of bulbs for fall planting of spring daffodils, tulips, irises, and day lilies. Mary also asked about planting some shrubs and bulbs in the plot of land beside the store, and maybe, even building a greenhouse to grow indoor plants from seeds for sale during the winter and next summer. They talked to the nursery owner about plans and details, but made no decisions. Mr. Davis asked Mary all kinds of questions about growing plants, fertilizing, preparing soil for garden, greenhouse, and potting plants. They bought some fertilizer, but planned to get composted manure from the farmers. They talked about their dreams, and about Mr. Davis' wife and child who had died in childbirth many years earlier. The general store had been his life, the East Bend Township customers his family.

They bought some geraniums and begonias—flats they could transplant into larger pots and bulbs to plant for blooms for house plants, and more flowering bushes for fall planting. Mary found she was singing to herself that week as she transplanted and fertilized the seedlings between customers.

Early Sunday morning, Mary Esther prepared the picnic. She had saved slices from the beef roast to make sandwiches, made deviled eggs, carrot and green pepper sticks, an apple pie, and a quart jar of lemonade made from rare lemons shipped from Florida, which she had bought from Mr. Davis. After she squeezed the lemons, she carefully saved the seeds. It would be interesting to grow a lemon tree. She also searched through her notebooks for her very first poem, written about the secret place she had found coming home from school one rainy day. She went back to the kitchen to put some left-over baked beans in a bowl. Men need more to eat than women, she decided.

Lincoln met her with a big smile and led her to the buggy. "Where to, Miss Mary?" he asked.

"We'll ride to Mr. Huthman's farm, and walk from there. I found this lovely place one very, very rainy day walking home from school. The footbridge over the creek was under water. Lucy and Stephen waded across, but I walked along the creek upstream until I found a place where I could step across from rock to rock. It was almost a mile, and I crossed into Huthman's pasture. I'll show you what I found. It's all right with Mr. Huthman. I asked permission."

"So we won't be caught trespassing. You are a proper lady, Mary." Lincoln laughed. "I didn't get permission from anyone when I was hunting that deer, or when I took you there." They parked the horse and buggy under a tree, and Lincoln picked up the basket. Mary put the blanket over her arm and led the way along a cornfield and a wheat field to the meadow bordered by a large grove of big trees beside the creek with the stepping stones. Under the shade of a gnarled, aged oak tree there was just enough room for the blanket.

Before they spread it, Mary pulled back the grass between the roots of the oak to reveal the bell blossoms of a lavender flower. "It's a false fox-glove, the first one I'd ever seen. Mother told me its name when I showed it to her. It's rare around here." Mary added, there are several kinds of wildflowers in this grove, ones that like the shade. The meadow we came through has lots more in different seasons."

"It is a special place, Mary, and even on a hot August day it's pleasantly cool. Let me spread that blanket, and get some water from the stream."

Mary handed him the blanket. "I made some lemonade, Lincoln. We can drink that first, and then get water if we want." Mary spread the food on a cloth, and handed Lincoln the beef sandwich as she put a plate before him and offered the beans, salad sticks and eggs, and poured lemonade in the glasses, carefully finding a very flat spot for each. After they had finished the picnic and cleared the blanket, Mary took the paper out of her pocket, and said, "Lincoln, I don't know whether you can stand poetry or not. There weren't many men in the

Athenaeum Society at Antioch, but I'm going to take a chance and read my very first poem, written the evening after I found this false foxglove."

"I'd really like to hear it, Mary. I learned to enjoy poetry studying English Literature and Shakespeare—and the Bible, too." Lincoln sat with crossed legs and listened intently as Mary read:

The False Foxglove

I found you growing in the wood
Beneath the gnarled and aged trees
Where shadows lay. In grass you stood
And bent toward me in the breeze.
My pulses leaped in glad surprise;
My fingers throbbed to clasp your stem.
I bent above love's longing eyes—
I plucked you. Let that one condemn
Who never down your waxen bell
Looked far and deep into your heart
And felt the joy he could not tell
Your form and loveliness impart.

Lincoln said softly, "It's beautiful." And after a few moments, he explained, "It lets me look into your heart and soul, too. Beauty speaks to us deep inside. I remember when I was six, and we were preparing to come from Zenia, Ohio, here to homestead, I wanted almost desperately to bring an ear of Indian corn. It was not anything like a flower, but I was fascinated with the various colors, and Father had let me help him plant a few hills of it. That fall I had harvested it, and made decorations to put on doors for my mother, my teacher, and two other grown-up friends. My mother helped me make a doll for my sister, and my brother helped me make a pipe for my father. The Indian corn was beautiful, and different, and my special project. I asked to bring an ear of it to Illinois. When Father said we had no room for unnecessary things, I was hurt and angry. I went into the house and banged the ear of corn against the sink, and grains flew all over the kitchen. I stooped down and scraped a handful of them off the floor and stuffed them into my pocket. I carried them there all the way to Illinois, and one day when Father was away, I planted them in the corner of the corn field."

"I like that story even more than the one about the big deer. It tells me about you. What did your father say when he found the Indian corn growing there? Was he angry?"

"No." Lincoln laughed again. "He didn't say anything about it until I brought in the harvest. Then he said, 'I didn't know how much it meant to you, Lincoln. I'm glad you found a way to bring the seeds.' He's a wonderful Father."

"We both have wonderful parents. We are blessed, aren't we? But you probably didn't have much time to play. I remember the joy of running through the meadows, playing games. There was one meadow with needles—a narrow, sharp seed on the long stem. We played with them. There's a slough going through one pasture nearer our house. We played in the water, gathered small stones—I still have some of them." After a thoughtful silence, Mary asked, "Do you want to pick a bouquet?"

"Not this time. Somehow the flowers here seem so right, so happy hiding in the grass. Let's leave them. I know why you like this grove. It seems almost sacred." After a moment, he added, "We have two more Sundays before you start teaching. Do you have any more favorite places?"

"Nothing secret. You choose." Mary wanted the Sundays to go on and on.

Sharing Sundays

The next Sunday, Lincoln took her to his farm to have Sunday dinner with his family. Mary already was friends with Emmet who worked with her at Mr. Davis' store, and had known Victoria and Wilbert at school, and, of course, the Green family at church, but she had never had a long conversation with Lincoln's parents. She immediately felt at ease with Augusta, sharing teaching experiences, gardening, and the pioneering experiences. Augusta asked Mary to describe the Crepe Myrtle bush again. It was doing well, but it was too soon to expect blooms. David Green told stories of his days in Xenia and on the trail giving them a humorous twist. Mary recognized the formal drawl Lincoln had used telling of the Big Deer.

After Mary had helped with the dishes, Lincoln took her arm and led her toward the chicken house he and Victoria had built of little logs, the lean-to, now with a fourth side, and then they walked to the little waterfall where Lincoln and Victoria had found the rocks for the foundation. The woods had been thinned quite a lot to build the house, but it was filling up with new growth, and Lincoln showed her the blackberry bushes that had given variety to their dried food the first summer before the gardens produced. Mary then asked to see the rest of the house they had built, and hear the stories of its building.

On the last Sunday before her school started, Mary invited him to have dinner with her family. Lincoln had known Julius and Artemissa Cranston since they returned to Gibson City when he was thirteen. He had admired Leslie, gone to school with Clara Jeanette, and known Mary as a playmate of Victoria's. But this time it was different. While the women were getting dinner on the table, Lincoln, after a few minutes of conversation with Julius in the library, asked, "Julius, I have heard you preach before we had a church on Sundays when the preacher's round took him to other towns. Did you have Seminary education like my father?"

"Yes, I studied in Mechanicsburg. I also went to Virginia and peddled door to door. But when I came to Illinois, first I bought 120 acres here with my father's help. Then I worked as a bricklayer in Clinton. In time, though, I decided to be a farmer. I believe farmers appreciate God. So many of Jesus' parables are about farming. I didn't really preach, but someone had to give some kind of teachings when we had no preacher. The Bible is full of good ideas."

"I remember your teachings. They were interesting and helpful," Lincoln commented. "I would like to be able to do it as well as you did. But I enjoy farming, too. Life and growth are a fascinating part of the mystery of God."

"Do you have a favorite Scripture?" Julius asked.

"Probably Psalm 137, the assurance that God is always with you, everywhere. Did you have one that helped you with the Sunday teachings?"

Julius responded, "I'm not sure exactly when I discovered the wonders of the Gospel of John: Verses 1, 2, and 14, but it changed my life. The first three words shout, 'Go to Genesis 1:1—In the Beginning.'"

Lincoln grasped the parallel, and quoted, "'In the beginning God created the heavens and the earth.' And 'In the beginning was the Word, and the Word was with God, and the Word was God.' And verse 2 in John proclaims that the Word created everything that was created. Yes, Julius, that is enough to build a life on."

Julius' eyes shone. "And there's more! Jesus and the Word are the same. When God said, 'Light, be!' that was His Word. The Word, Jesus, brought the Light of God into the world he had created, and created our sun, life, and everything else.'"

"'And the Word became flesh and dwelt among us.' Yes, yes. I have always treasured God's Word, but now I will honor it even more. Thank you for sharing this with me, Julius." Lincoln sat a while in silence to contemplate, and then commented, "You worked in a brickyard. That was harder than farming."

"Yes," Julius answered. "But it earns more ready cash. I met Artemissa, married her, and came here to farm for a couple of years, and then went back to Ford County. Mary was just one year old when we left. Then in 1876 I decided to go to Kansas to homestead. I sold our land in Ford County, and came back here and sold those 120 acres. But before we were ready to set out, Artemissa's father died. Artemissa and I decided then to stay here to take care of her mother, and farm their land. It was a good decision."

"My grandfather came from England to Pennsylvania, then to Ohio. He's still there, with most of my aunts and uncles. But my father and mother decided that the free land under the Homestead Act was too good an opportunity to miss." Lincoln added, "It is better here than on our rented farm in Ohio."

Before Julius could comment, Artemissa came to call them to dinner. The table was filled with appetizing dishes. As they ate, there were stories of wagon trains, and building farms from prairies, and homes from raw timber, days of home school, and one-room schools, growing crops and flowers, floods, and stories about college days past and anticipation of the future. Lucy Roxanne—usually called Lucy—had wonderful tales to tell of earlier days, and her childhood and marriage in Vermont.

Lucy insisted Mary show Lincoln her flower garden instead of helping with the dishes. Lincoln was properly impressed, and they wandered around the farm, sharing trivialities. Then Lincoln asked, "Mary, teaching school won't take all your time on Sundays, will it?"

"Maybe not." She looked at him. "I'll not let it."

The Sunday afternoons changed from picnics to strolls through autumn woods, gathering nuts, or long conversations before a warm fire. Mary Esther found teaching more satisfying than she had expected. Each child was special, with struggles and surprises. The upper classes learned by helping the younger, and Mary found time to teach some botany in the autumn color hiding beneath the green leaves, and the new leaves forming in the bumps of buds on the twigs while the life-giving sap retreated to the warmer roots. They rooted twigs and planted bulbs. But of course, the focus was on basics. Her Saturdays were her favorites, because Mr. Davis had persuaded her to spend them in the little greenhouse in his store. She had the best of both worlds.

Lincoln found time, after his father's and his own crops were harvested and fields cleared for spring plowing, to work on repairing fences and buildings, and caring for the animals. He was also reading his Bible, books from the Cranston library, and keeping a journal.

During the Christmas break Mary worked half days for Mr. Davis, developed lesson plans for the spring term, but at Lincoln's insistence, saved time to be with him. She had knitted a scarf, hat, and gloves for Lincoln as her Christmas gift. Lincoln had found in a catalog a book of colored pictures of wild flowers, all described and identified. Both were delighted. Lincoln wore the gifts in their winter walks. But on Wednesday and Thursday after Christmas, a blizzard pre-empted all activity. On Friday, Mary went home from Mr. Davis' store early, and found Lincoln and his brother Wilbert in the front yard with Lucy helping the younger children build a family of snowmen. Stephen—eight—his brown curls showing beneath his red stocking cap, was rolling snowballs, proud of his strength. Grace—five, and Artie—three were having fun starting the snowballs in their hands, and trying to roll them in crooked lines. With a scarf tied over her blond curls, Lucy gently turned them to keep them round. Lincoln and Wilbert lifted middle-sized balls on top of a big balls, and while they placed the heads on top, Lucy went inside to get carrots for noses, walnuts for eyes, and slices of red pepper for mouths. Mary took in the scene, and went inside to change quickly and grab hats for the various snow-family members, and some old work gloves to put on stick-arms for the papa. Then she grabbed a red polka-dot scarf and a broom for the snow mama. Lincoln disappeared for a few moments and returned with an improvised corncob pipe for the papa, and a forked twig slingshot for the snow boy. Grace picked some dry berries from a dogwood tree for buttons, and helped Artie put them onto the snowman's chest. He stepped back and clapped, laughing with glee. They all clapped and laughed, and named the snow family crazy names. Stephen started throwing snowballs at them. Mary Esther said, "Wait, Stephen. Let's call Mother and Father to come see."

Stephen ran to the house, and returned soon with Julius and Artemissa Cranston, and almost pulling the hand of his grandmother Lucy Atwood. As she stood admiring the snowmen, Artemissa said, "It looks as if we have five more guests for dinner. What a lovely family!"

Julius listened carefully as Stephen introduced them, "Popperjack, Sweepormiss, Slinger, Cookie, and Littlebit Snow."

Father Julius bowed as he said, "It's a pleasure to meet you. Welcome." Then he turned to Lincoln and Wilbert, and added, "They're masterpieces. What a lot of work!"

"It was fun. We all had a part. You should have seen how well the children rolled those balls and found ways to make them into people. Even Artie and Grace added their touch."

After admiring the snowmen, they all went inside to sit by the fire to warm their fingers and toes. Lincoln, remembering, said, "When I was six, on our way from Ohio in the covered wagons, we had to stop for a terrible blizzard. A strong wind blew lots and lots of snow around us for three days. We couldn't even see to go from the wagon to the fire in the center of the corral. Father and my older brothers had to help clear snow from the grass so the cattle could feed. Mother told us stories and taught us lessons, all crowded in the covered wagon. I was just one year older than Grace."

"Did you make snowmen then?" Grace asked?

"It was too windy even to stand for more than a moment. But after the storm stopped, we younger boys threw a few snowballs as we walked beside the wagons in the snow."

After they were warm, Lincoln suggested that he and Wilbert take Mary and Lucy for a sleigh ride. He had rented a sleigh from the stable. They put on their warmest clothes, and Mary brought a blanket for each. What fun they had, laughing and singing Christmas Carols and folk songs. Mary said that tree limbs lined with snow, and white snow blankets, even on shacks, looked as if Gibson City was gift-wrapped. They went past Grandfather Cranston's house just to wave and call out hello. They didn't stay out long enough to get chilled, but when they returned, Lincoln offered to take the children for a short ride. Lucy and Mary thought they should go, too, to hold Grace and Artie. The children were delighted and excited to glide over the white roads in the white world. After a few moments, Mary noticed Lincoln was coughing. "Just a bit too long in the winter air," he said." Mary insisted he and Wilbert stay for supper to get really warm before they started home. There was always room at their family table for guests, and always enough food to share.

The youth class had a square dance party to welcome in the New Year. Wilbert again came with Lincoln to escort Lucy. Lincoln had invited Mary. Mary wondered how long Lucy had been seeing Wilbert. Maybe it was time to have a sisterly confidential talk. Celebrating with long-time friends was a perfect way to start 1888. But the next day was time for Mary to start teaching. This vacation had been the most special time in her life, but she wondered why Lincoln never mentioned anything about plans for the future.

Mary kept very busy during the spring semester, and the bright spring gardens of farms and town were a delight and satisfaction. Mr. Davis was learning more and more what to stock and how to care for it. He talked about getting a full-time assistant for the store so that he could partially retire in a year or two to tend to the garden center. Mary half-way wished he could find a widow to marry to keep him company. He would make a very good husband, and deserved a bit of happiness. He must be at least as old as her grandfather. He was one of the first settlers.

Lincoln found the winter damp and cold, and could hardly wait for spring and the heat of summer. His cough was not going away. Even sitting in front of the fireplace helped only a little. However, with the spring weather and time spent outdoors in preparing and planting the spring crops, the cough disappeared.

Summer was a wonderful time. Lincoln and Mary hunted wild flowers pictured in the book he had given her for Christmas, and Mary kept a list of each one they found. After getting the fall orders ready, Mary began another year of teaching. She was saving most of her salary, and she knew exactly what she wanted to do. She would go back to school! When she mentioned that to Lincoln he said, "I understand, Mary. For years I've been wanting to go to Seminary, but my father really needs me to help with the farm."

All through the next school year, Mary helped Mr. Davis on Saturdays, and taught her students during the week, but Sunday afternoons were always with Lincoln. He was careful to keep warm, but also to spend time outdoors in the fresh air, never allowing himself to get chilled. His cough was not nearly as bad as the previous year.

In late July of 1889, Lincoln met Mary for their Sunday picnic after church with a letter in his hand. When they were in the buggy, he handed it to Mary to read. "Dear Father and Mother, If it is all right with you, my wife and I would like to come back to East Bend Township and help you with the farm," she read, "We have had a good offer for our land here in Ohio, and know your farm is too large for one man to farm. It's time Lincoln was free to go to Seminary, as has been his dream."

It took Mary a few moments to think through all that those few words meant. "Lincoln, now you really are free to go to seminary, aren't you? You do feel the call to be a pastor, don't you? Your talks to the youth group have been inspired. What are your plans?"

Lincoln answered slowly, "The Reverend Ezra Fox—you remember him, don't you?—often encouraged me to go into the ministry, but my father needed me. Now that John is will be here to help Father, I'm considering training for that. Leslie was so enthusiastic about Adrian College, and it has a good Seminary. I am thinking about writing to see if they will admit me in September. It's been so long since I finished high school. It may be too late for a new career."

Mary hid her disappointment at the thought of Lincoln being far away in Michigan, and perhaps starting a new life with no place in it for her. "Lincoln, you have kept your mind active with reading, and your heart right with God. If He has called you to be a pastor, then it's the right thing to do to go to seminary." After a moment, she added, "If it is God's plan, then the college will accept you."

A Year to Learn

And Adrian College did accept Lincoln. In August, Lincoln was busy getting ready for college, and helping with harvesting until he drove to pick up John and his wife at the station the last day of August. Sunday afternoons were full of his dreams and plans. Mary had decided not to teach another year. Mr. Davis was doing very well with the garden center, and it was time for Mary to think about her future. She did not want to spend the rest of her life teaching in a one-room school in her home town. To find another career, or teach in a more challenging grade would require more education. She had saved enough money for at least one more year of college. But what about Lincoln, she wondered. After dinner, she drew Lucy aside.

"Lucy, Lincoln is going to Adrian College for Seminary, and I've been wondering if Wilbert has said anything to you about what Lincoln plans for the future."

Lucy looked at Mary's eyes, filling with tears. "Oh, Mary, hasn't he said anything to you about how he feels about you? It's been more than two years, he's been seeing you every Sunday, and he looks at you so fondly. Wilbert hasn't said anything about his brother's intentions toward you, but he has hinted that he is thinking of plans for us.

Mary, I don't know. Some men never marry."

"Well, Lucy, it's time I faced it. I have to build a life on my own. The University of Illinois is accepting women this year, and I'm going to enroll and specialize in art."

"Why art, Mary? It's not practical." Lucy had no appreciation for art or flowers.

"Lucy, life is empty without beauty. What the world needs is the refining influence of art, not only in the picture galleries accessible to a few, but in all the affairs of our daily life.

"There's not time in our lives for unnecessary things. What does art do to help us?" Lucy was thinking of how busy her parents and grandparents always were.

Mary tried to explain, "Art lifts us from drudgery and toil, and from selfish desire, up to those things which are truly beautiful, giving us insight into nature and nature's God. It is a religious duty to be happy."

"My, Mary! You are a deep thinker. I don't see how studying art, though, will help you build a productive life?" Lucy's face reflected worry about her sister.

"I'll take other courses, too, so that I can get a teaching position in a larger school, and maybe teach art, or botany in addition to basic courses like English, history, and literature." My four years of teaching experience should help me find a good position. And whatever I do, I'll have the benefit of art in my life." Mary was getting more enthusiastic about another year of college.

As she packed her suitcase, she looked through her books from Antioch. It had been a good year. In the fly-leafs, she reread the words of wisdom that had impressed her enough to preserve them in her books. "Truth, to be taught, must be oft taught." (March 30, 1887). "The teacher who gets through only half a lesson is only half a teacher." She thought about her four years of teaching. She had tried to teach truth, and tried to finish her planned lessons. "There is no school that deepens the mind and broadens thought like contact with mankind." The University of Illinois might be a good place to improve her mind. She sang to herself as she closed the small trunk of clothes.

In September of 1889, Mary Esther Cranston enrolled in the University of Illinois. She found a room near the campus, with Lucy and Stella George, as her roommates. She was a student in a business school. Mary Esther scheduled her classes in the Art Department, taking oil painting and pottery, as well as advanced botany and world history. It was so natural to be learning again. Much more enjoyable than teaching.

It was the first year the University had admitted women, and there were not very many women in her classes, and even though she knew she was not beautiful like Lucy, many of her fellow students showed interest in her. For several weeks, Mary ignored them, but after a month or so she began making friends with several. They were away from home, too, and many in her art courses had interests in common. Some in her botany class asked her for help. She reasoned, if Lincoln was not interested in a future with her, she might as well be a little open to get to know other men—but there were none like Lincoln.

During the Christmas vacation, Lincoln was suffering from coughing, and there was only one Sunday afternoon together. After church they ate dinner with Mary's parents and grandmother Roxanna Atwood, and then sat by the fire. They shared college experiences. Lincoln was excited about his study of the Bible, and his introduction to the Greek Language. "Did you know, Mary, that

Hebrew and Greek are the only languages that have letters of the alphabet as numbers? My Greek professor told us one afternoon that each number has a specific meaning, such as 6 is the number of man, created on the sixth day, and 4 the number of nature, with the four seasons and the four directions and winds, etc. 1 is unity, and 2 division. He said also that key words in the Bible have letters that add up to a multiple of the number of their meaning. I wished he had gone into it more thoroughly. I'd like to know more about that. There's so much more to learn about the Bible, Mary. One could spend a lifetime and never know it all. Of course, I need to focus on Jesus and His salvation message." Lincoln was silent for a few moments, and then asked, "I've heard you are studying oil painting and pottery Are you planning to be an artist?"

"Probably not, Lincoln. But I am learning to appreciate the talents of those who are. It's not as easy as it seems. I'm learning how to show distance by perspective, placement on the canvas and shading of colors, how to have a focal point and avoid dividing the canvas in half. And I can mix colors pretty well. I've learned to use a pottery wheel, but not perfectly. It's more interesting to mold with my hands, but I have to practice a lot more to do that well." Mary looked at her hands a moment, and added, "I believe I could teach children a little about art, or will be able by the end of the spring classes."

"You have always seen things around with an eye to beauty, like an artist. Your flower arrangements and plantings were artistic. You would probably make a good artist." Lincoln remembered her work with Mr. Davis and their summer picnics.

"I believe that art in ones life enriches the spiritual aspects of life, relieving the monotony of constant work. I'm practical, too. I'm taking botany and world history. If I have to teach, I'll be well prepared."

"Are you planning to teach again?" Lincoln looked at his hands as he asked.

"Lincoln, I don't know. I don't want to be a burden to my parents, but I don't really want to teach in a one-room school any more. Maybe advanced courses somewhere—I'd like to teach ideas, to help children think." Mary Esther had a flicker of hope when Lincoln looked up. His blue eyes searching her face. "What are your plans, Lincoln? How long is the seminary course?"

"Two years, Mary. I hope to receive a call to a United Brethren Church when I finish." Then Lincoln said under his breath, "If I finish."

Mary gasped. "What?"

"Nothing." Then he added, "Sometimes I just worry about this cough." He looked up. "It's already dark, Mary. I have to get home." Lincoln put on his coat and left, saying a brief goodbye.

With a heavy heart, Mary returned to Urbana for the spring semester. The campus was different this semester. Students were unhappy with the faculty's idea that discipline was paramount. A few leaders were talking about the need to focus on the idea of freedom, since the Declaration of Independence emphasized that. Mary Esther was uneasy with the unrest and spirit of conflict among the students. Near the end of the school year, President Peabody, yielding to the student pressures, resigned. Of course, Mary Esther believed in freedom, but she also knew that discipline was necessary. She was troubled by the unrest, and pondered ways to accomplish change without conflict. She wrote on the fly-leaf of her history book, "Reform can only be affected by reformers, and reformers must be enthusiastic." Charles Johnson was enthusiastic. He was one of the campus leaders in the movement for more freedom. "But is that the college's job?"

She added, "There is no school that disciplines the mind and broadens thought like contact with mankind." (Ella Wheeler.)

Mary had been seeing Charles Johnson, whom she had met in her history class. They had attended some concerts together. She was a good listener as he explained why the students wanted more freedom. She enjoyed the evenings, with lovely music, and found his conversation stimulating. He was studying technical machines, and was fascinated with trains, cotton gins, thrashing machines, and anything with power to help man's work. He talked about the industrial revolution in Europe changing the civilized world. But Charles was absorbed in himself, his learning, and his radical ideas and plans to invent more machines and get rich. When Mary called his attention to a rainbow after a rain storm, he looked, and said, "Oh, yes. It's pretty, isn't it?" But then went back to describing a steam engine he was working on. He was just like the men she knew in school in Ohio. Lincoln would have reached for her hand, stood with her watching, admiring, and treasuring the shared beauty until it faded away. There he was again. She couldn't get Lincoln out of her thoughts—or out of her heart.

Jason Van Klassen from her oil painting class asked her to have dinner with him one evening, but then he asked her to pose for him in his quarters. Of course she refused. Mary Esther concentrated on her studies, looking forward to summer vacation. Even if there was no future with him, it would be good to see Lincoln, and maybe share those Sundays again.

When Lincoln arrived home from Adrian, the Sunday picnics resumed. Mary found that it was so natural and easy to be with him, discovering new secret places and reveling in the original ones. If that was all there was to be, she would enjoy every moment and every memory.

Plans for Two

With the warm days of summer, Lincoln's mood was exuberant, and by the Fourth of July he planned an all-day picnic at Mary's secret place. They waded in the stream, skipping flat stones, and walked barefoot on the meadow grass, laughing. Mary stepped on a stone and almost lost her balance. Quickly, Lincoln caught her, and holding her tight, kissed her. Mary Esther put her arms around his neck and looked into his eyes, smiling.

"You must know, Mary, that I've been hopelessly in love with you since our very first picnic. No, even before that, when you were telling me about that wonderful Crepe Myrtle tree. It had a few blooms last year, and they're as lovely as you described. But, Mary, I couldn't tell you. I know I had some problem with my lungs, and I couldn't ask you to marry a sick man, and I couldn't give up seeing you. Maybe—I've been better this year—maybe you would consider taking a chance and marrying me. I'd understand if you wouldn't—"

Mary's heart skipped a beat as she interrupted, "Lincoln, I've been wondering why you never talked about the future, a future that for me, would be empty without you. I've never been so happy as when we're together."

"Then I'll never leave you." Lincoln took both her hands in his and said solemnly, "Miss Mary Esther Cranston, will you do me the honor of becoming my wife?"

"Mr. Lincoln Hamlin Green, I would be proud to be Mrs. Lincoln Hamlin Green."

Lincoln kissed her again and held her tighter. "How soon can we be married? Next Sunday?"

"Maybe a little longer to let Mother plan a wedding. She would be upset if we didn't invite family and friends. But what about your Seminary?"

"You'll go with me, of course. You can take classes, too."

"Oh, Lincoln, I would like that. When do classes start?" Mary was excited, already planning the most wonderful day of her life.

"On Monday, September 15th. I'll write my landlady to ask her to make room for the two of us. You'll like her, Mary, and she will be so happy for us. She worried about me last year, because I was alone so much." Lincoln could see in his mind Mrs. Henderson welcoming Mary into her home. And then he thought about the years ahead. "Mary Esther, it may not be easy to be a preacher's wife."

Mary Esther laughed. "Or a farmer's wife, or a teacher's wife? Lincoln, life isn't ever really easy, but if we're together, I'll welcome any challenge. And God will be with us. I like people and will find ways to serve."

"How soon can we be married, Mary? I've wasted so many years." Lincoln's eyes pleaded.

"Soon, Lincoln. I've waited so long for you to ask. I'll talk with my parents about plans. Do you think the Reverend Fox could perform the ceremony? We've both been impressed with his faith and wisdom."

"Yes, Mary. He's the one who encouraged me to go to Seminary. I'll arrange it with him as soon as you tell me the date." Lincoln was fumbling with something in his hand, and reached over and placed a clover ring on her finger. "I'll soon have the real one, Mary Esther." Mary leaned over and kissed him on the cheek, and he pulled her to him and kissed her again.

When Lincoln reluctantly took Mary Esther home that evening, they held hands as they stood before Julius and Artemissa.

Artemissa greeted them, saying, "I can tell from your eyes something wonderful has happened. Tell us."

Lincoln said, "Yes. Mary Esther has agreed to marry me. Mr. Cranston, I'm asking for your blessing and permission to marry your daughter."

Julius laughed as he shook Lincoln's hand and said, "Gladly. We know Mary Esther will be loved and cared for with you. You two lovers belong together."

Artemissa took both of Lincoln's hands and smiled as she said, "Welcome to our family, Lincoln."

"Mother, Lincoln's school starts September 15, and he wants me to take classes, too. We don't need a fancy wedding, but we know our families will want to share in our joy." Then Mary added, "Lincoln and I would like Reverend Ezra Fox to perform the wedding ceremony, if that's possible."

Julius said, "He's preaching at the Sibley church now. We'll write to ask him when he can come."

"I hope it's soon. Maybe August first." Lincoln said. "I'd like time for a long honeymoon before we have to leave for college."

But that wasn't to be. The first free date the Reverend Ezra Fox had was September 10. That meant no time at all for a honeymoon—or maybe one day.

On Monday, Mary Esther went to tell her grandfather Cranston the news. He hugged her, and reminded her of their talk after she had returned from college and Clara Jeanette and Leslie had both left for their new lives. "You had no idea what you wanted to do with your life. You considered teaching, and said you didn't want to do that as a career. You said you'd like to be a student and learn more and more, and you had thought there was no chance for marriage. Mary Esther, you're getting all three choices! It seems to me God is watching over you very carefully." His grin turned into a little wrinkle between his eyes as he added, "What about Lincoln's cough, Mary? I was wondering if he had tuberculosis."

"That's why he waited so long to ask me to marry him. He didn't think it was right for him to ask me to marry a sick man. But he was better last winter, and he did tell me of his reluctance, and suggest I not take the chance. But, Grandfather, if you love a person, you want to share his life even if it is difficult. You would have married Grandmother, wouldn't you, even if she might have had a possible problem?" Mary Esther knew he would not hesitate.

"Yes, I would have wanted to take care of her. And I knew, dear Mary, how you wondered why Lincoln had not asked you to marry him sooner. You wanted him to, and you knew, somehow, that he loved you. But, my dear Mary Esther, if he does have tuberculosis, you must be careful not to catch it, and expect some difficulties."

"I know, Grandfather. And I want to be with him anyway. He loves me, and loves the things I love. We share the love of God's beauty, and trust in our loving Father God. He will be a wonderful preacher, and I will be proud to be his wife." Mary paused, and added, "I would be proud to be his wife if he were a farmer, too."

"I know that, too. I give you my blessing, and my prayers. Lincoln is a good man, and will be a good husband for my very special granddaughter."

The weeks passed quickly. Mary decided to wear the sky-blue dress she had made for Clara Jeanette's wedding, and Lucy, as bridesmaid, made her dress a darker blue. There would be more friends invited, in addition to the large family. Grandmother Atwood was confident that September 10th would be a bright and sunny fall day, still warm enough to have the reception on her large lawn.

As a student, Mary decided, she did not need a new wardrobe. She carefully chose her favorite clothes, thinking of the colder winters at Adrian. There would be one small trunk shipped, and a small suitcase to carry on the train. Lincoln had planned a one-day honeymoon in Chicago. The Sunday picnics were treasured times of planning and nostalgia. After Seminary, they would be assigned a church somewhere, but Sundays would belong to the congregation.

September 10th was, as Grandma Atwood had predicted, a lovely early fall day. Roxanne had prepared a trellis covered with roses for the bride and groom in the large side yard, with the many chairs from the house and improvised benches for the guests. Improvised tables were ready in the back yard by the garden for the simple reception.

Early in the morning, Mary Esther took the blue dress from the closet, and decided to try it on before she ironed out the wrinkles. She went into her mother's room to ask her to button the row of buttons in back. Roxanne pulled and pulled, and finally got those all buttoned. Mary Esther said, in panic, "Mother, I can't breathe. I'm fatter! I can't wear this, and I don't have anything else nice enough to wear." Tears of frustration filled her eyes.

"Don't fret, Mary. This is easy to fix, and we have plenty of time before the wedding" Her mother started unbuttoning the dress as she added, "All we have to do is rip some of the darts and press it. I'll take care of it."

Just as Lucy finished buttoning the many buttons on the back of Mary Esther's dress, now a perfect fit, Grandma Atwood came into the room. She gave her a gentle hug, saying, "What a beautiful bride! I'll miss you, Mary Esther. I've watched you grow from a curious, bright little girl into a talented, dedicated teacher, an eager student, and now ready to start a new life as wife of a fine man. You will be a great help to a preacher! Here is a little remembrance of me to wear as you stand before that preacher friend, and for the rest of your life." She pinned the broach, an opal surrounded by tiny pearls outlined in gold filigree, at the lace collar, as she added, "This came from England. My husband gave it to me in Vermont for our twenty-fifth wedding anniversary. Let it remind you of how much I love you, always." Mary Esther had tears in her eyes as she hugged her grandmother. "There, there, don't cry on your wedding day."

Waiting for the scheduled time, Mary Esther, dressed comfortably in the blue dress with the opal pin on the collar, peeked from her bedroom window as the guests arrived. There were so many friends and she loved every one of them. Lucy was with her, combing Mary's blond hair over and over to get it just perfect. Lucy's hair was darker with blond highlights, and her darker lashes and brows accented her dark blue eyes set in a delicate face with ivory skin and a slightly pointed chin. She was the beauty of the family, but today she was intent on bringing out the glow in Mary's eyes and face. "Mary," she said, "pinch your cheeks to make them pink, and press your lips together. There, that blue dress is just right color for you. You're beautiful today."

Lucy went to the window, too, watching guests arriving. "Here they come, Mary. Lincoln is taller than Wilbert. I hadn't noticed how much, before. But you're taller than I am, too. They're both so handsome. I like the way they walk, shoulders back, heads held high. Mary, you can tell from the way people greet them. Everybody likes them. And isn't their mother a very special woman? You're going to get along beautifully with your in-laws."

"I know, Lucy. They are so close together. The two oldest boys stayed to work to help pay for the big house they built, and they all worked together to cut the logs, gather stones for the foundation –Lincoln, Victoria, and Melissa did that—and build it themselves. John has even moved back to help his father. Of course, Wilbert was too young to do anything, but when he got old enough, he was a big help, too." Mary thought a moment, and added, "Mrs. Green even helped cut down trees with the cross saw, and hold boards in place to nail. And what I like best about her is the way she taught not only her own children, but the neighbor children, too, before Gibson City built their school. And she kept up her big garden. I hope I can be as good a wife and Mother as she is."

Lucy gave Mary a gentle hug, trying not to wrinkle her dress. "Of course you can, Mary. You are a wonderful gardener, a teacher, and an artist, and I don't know anyone who is as ingenuous as you are finding ways to make things work. You're certainly not lazy. I can't work half as fast and well as you do. Lincoln's a lucky man."

"I'll do my best." For a brief moment Mary thought about the tuberculosis, but not long. Lincoln was everything she had longed for in her husband, strong and tender, educated, and yet modest. He full of faith, willing to work, and laugh, and enjoy beauty.

Mary's mother came to the door, and looked at her two daughters.

She kissed Mary on the cheek. "You're glowing, and lovely, Mary. Lincoln will be so proud of you. He's ready and waiting, and your grandfather is ready too. Lucy, you look pretty enough to be a bride, too. It's time."

Reverend Fox greeted Lincoln warmly, "I was wondering how long it would take you two to get together. You were made for each other." It was a simple wedding. Lucy held the bouquet of flowers beside Mary Esther, while Wilbert, standing beside Lincoln, held the wide gold wedding band until it was time for Lincoln to put it on Mary's finger. As Lincoln placed it on her finger, he whispered, "See, I promised."

After the vows, Reverend Fox gave a short prayer asking God to bless this union, to lead and care for them, and have them prosper throughout their lives. During the reception, he took Lincoln aside to say, "I hear you're attending Seminary at Adrian. Good school. I always thought you had a call from God to preach."

Lincoln was enthusiastic as he explained, "I did feel a call, Reverend Fox, but I had to wait until John came home to help Father. I'm finding the deeper meanings in the Bible challenging and fascinating. I'm looking forward to ministry. I have been speaking to the youth group occasionally. You are the one who inspired and encouraged me. Thank you."

"And you've chosen a good helpmate, too." Reverend Fox shook Lincoln's hand and held it a little longer. "May God bless you both, and give you health, long life, and a loving family."

"Thank you for adding 'health,' Reverend. I've had a worrisome cough at times."

"We'll pray for your healing, Lincoln. God answers prayers." Reverend Fox moved through the guests greeting those he remembered from his ministry in Gibson City.

After the reception line, Lincoln and Mary were careful to speak to every friend and family member, knowing they might not have a chance to see many of them again. They were close friends, part of their growing-up years, part of their lives. Mr. Davis lingered longer and Mary Esther took his hand, saying, “You gave me a new lease on life when I was discouraged, Mr. Davis. I will never forget the joy of beginning the flower department in your store, and the pleasure of the time we spent together. I learned more from you about planning and organizing than I taught you about those plants. I’ll never forget you. Thank you.”

Mr. Davis smiled as he remembered. “You gave me more than you knew. The flower department has been my joy and fulfillment. It’s still my favorite part of the store. Mary Esther, keep on sharing your appreciation of beauty. People need that in their lives.”

“I will, Mr. Davis.” Mary answered. “I can’t help it. It’s a big part of me. Thank you, dear friend.”

After the guests had left, Mary found Lucy still talking with Wilbert, and said, “Come, help me change to my travel clothes.” In their room, Mary changed to a skirt and white blouse, wearing the ivory pin Grandma Atwood had given her for her wedding dress, and carefully packing the blue dress on top of the travel case. She would wear it in Chicago if the occasion was right. “Lucy,” Mary said when the travel case was closed and ready, “Will I be able to be with you at your wedding? I can guess it’s not going to be too long.”

“He’s going to graduate from college first; that’s another year. We haven’t talked about a date, but I’ll be sure it’s at time when you can be matron of honor. I’m going to miss you, Mary.” Lucy closed the suitcase, and carried it to the bedroom door. “I know you’ll be happy, being married to Lincoln, and going to school both!"

"It's more than I dreamed of, Lucy. God plans for me were better than mine." Mary Esther picked up the suitcase.

"Mary," Lucy called, "Don't forget your coat! Lincoln told me to remind you you'd need it in Chicago." Mary Esther laughed, took the coat from Lucy, and headed down the stairs where Lincoln was waiting.

As he took the suitcase, Lincoln said, "Your grandfather insisted on taking his carriage so he and your grandmother could be with your parents and us as we drive to the train. I think he doesn't want to let you go." Lincoln, laughed. "But you're mine now, for always."

"Yes, for always. But Grandfather will still be dear to me, too.

Making Memories as One

The long drive to the train station was full of reminiscences, as if each one was trying to preserve in memory every special moment, and wishes and dreams about the future. As they reached the station, Artemissa handed Mary Esther a knitting bag, saying, "You didn't eat much at the wedding reception, so I packed a little sampling for you two."

"I'm too happy to be hungry now, but we probably will be before long. Thank you, Mother." Mary Esther kissed her on the cheek and held her hand a moment as she took the bag in with her valise.

At exactly 12:46 p.m., right on schedule, the train pulled into the station, black smoke trailing from the smokestack. Mary Esther remembered her arrival at that same station four years earlier, so uncertain of what she wanted to do with her life. Now there were no doubts. After the happy and tearful goodbyes, Lincoln helped Mary climb the steps into the train and turned to take the suitcases from Julius Cranston. The porter placed them in the rack, and Mary sat by the window with Lincoln next to her, waving to her parents and grandparents as the train pulled away.

As the train rattled along the track in rhythm, they watched the farms and little towns pass. Nearing Chicago, Lincoln asked, "Is this area familiar? It's near Ford County, I believe."

"It doesn't look much different from all the other farms and villages we've passed, but it could be. I might recognize the school or church we went to, but they weren't on the railroad track. I remember it was a nice place to live. But, Lincoln, Adrian will be a nice place to live, too. Tell me about it."

"Adrian is a college town, not too big, built around the campus. There are trees along the streets, but not much open space. We'll have two rooms in Mrs. Johnson's home, upstairs in the front of the house. She wrote that she was excited about my bringing a wife this year, and reserved my room and the one next to it for a sitting room. They're not fancy, Mary, but you'll like Mrs. Henderson. My room was on the southeast corner, where the morning sun would wake me. But you can pull the shade if you want to sleep." Lincoln went on to describe the other students and the fine meals, and then described the campus.

The train approached Chicago, and Mary looked to see signs of the big Chicago fire she had heard about when she was just beginning school. There were no signs of it, just buildings crowded together along street after street. Hardly any trees. When she caught a glimpse of Lake Michigan, she gasped. She had never seen an expanse of water with no shore on the other side. It was late afternoon when the train pulled into the station. Lincoln hailed one of the line of buggies for hire, announced, "The Palmer House."

"Yes Sir!" said the cab driver, tipping his hat. They drove North along Lake Michigan and then headed to a large, elegant building. Lincoln paid and tipped the driver, and a porter carried the suitcases into the lobby. It was beautiful, with marble and velvet. As he registered at the desk, Lincoln asked, "How far is it to the lake front, and is there a little park near it?"

"It's just about five blocks, and yes, there is a little park just a bit north."

Their room was comfortable with a fireplace. Lincoln placed Mary's suitcase on the bench provided and said, "Mary, let's take that knitting bag of wedding treats, and have a picnic by Lake Michigan."

"A picnic! Lincoln, what a wonderful way to begin our life together! I'll never forget our first picnic, and all those wonderful Sundays. After that reception, I thought I'd never be hungry again, but I am, a little." Mary answered. "Let me hang up my blue dress first, and I'll be ready."

"Don't forget your coat. It will be chilly by the lake."

They walked down unfamiliar sidewalks along busy streets and crowded tall buildings for a few blocks until they caught sight of Lake Michigan. There were some boats and ships along the dock, and just a block north was the little park. Lincoln led Mary to a bench facing the Lake. As the sunset reflected a golden glow on the sails of the boats and washed over the expanse of blue water tipped with gold, Mary Esther opened a package from the knitting bag to find two pieces of their wedding cake. She sighed in contentment as they savored the cake, the precious memories, and their dreams for the future.

There was a fire in the fireplace and a pitcher of hot water on the wash stand when they returned to their room. It was a wedding night to remember. The next morning, after breakfast in the hotel, they explored the downtown store windows and wandered through a few stores, but didn't buy anything. They had lunch in a German coffee shop, and Lincoln urged Mary to get a souvenir. In a china shop, Mary saw a tiny tray, white with a gold rim and a gold flower pattern, and on the back, a drawing of a king and two attendants and the words, "Royal Ironstone China, W.R. Grindley & CP." It's a perfect souvenir, Lincoln. Gold for the sunset, royal for the elegant honeymoon, the gold flower to remind us of our picnics, and useful to safely hold the lovely broach my grandmother gave me."

At 3:00 p.m. Lincoln had a surprise in store. They walked again to the beach. Lincoln took two tickets from his pocket and led Mary to the dock to board a small cruise ship for a steamboat ride on Lake Michigan. Mary understood, then, why she had brought a coat. Even with a bright sun, the breeze was quite chilly. They watched the shoreline disappear, felt the waves gently rocking the ship. Sometimes, they noted, the waves were not so gentle. Lincoln held Mary's arm securely until she became accustomed to the rhythm and changing slants of the deck. As the ship turned and headed back toward the dock, Mary squeezed Lincoln's hand. "It's beautiful, exciting, and sort of peaceful, all at the same time. The waves are fascinating and mesmerizing. Thank you for giving me this memory with you to treasure."

To complete their brief honeymoon, Lincoln had scheduled dinner in the elegant dining room of the Palmer House. "Put on that beautiful blue dress, Mary, and you'll be the most glorious lady there." Lincoln had to help with the buttons in back. The dinner in the formal dining room, served by uniformed waiters, was delicious and like a dream. She thought of the song from *The Bohemian Girl,* "I dreamt I dwelt in Marble Halls, with vassals and serfs by my side." And there was music from a string trio to give new memories.

Early the next morning they hired a carriage to take them to the train station, and were off to Adrian to register for their college classes.

Part II

Mr. and Mrs. Lincoln H. Green

Their First Home

As Lincoln helped Mary down the train steps, he noticed Mr. Henderson smiling as he came toward them. He put down the suitcases to shake his hand, saying, "How nice of you to come to meet us. I'm proud to introduce you to my wife, Mary. Mary, this is our landlord, Mr. Henderson."

Mary offered her hand to the husky man, looking into a smile showing broken teeth, but sparkling brown eyes surrounded by curling grey hair. "I'm very glad to meet you, Mr. Henderson. Lincoln has told me how fortunate he has been to find a room with you and Mrs. Henderson."

"He's told us about you. I'm so glad you said 'Yes.' He'd be lost without you. Welcome. Mrs. Henderson has enjoyed arranging a place for you two. Harold is already here. I have Nellie, here." He picked up one of the suitcases and led the way to the buggy.

With a flourish, he pulled a footstool from the back seat and placed it for Mary. She made a little curtsy and let him help her up. "Thank you, kind Sir."

He chatted with Lincoln as they drove down tree-shaded streets to a grey frame house with a porch across the front. After Lincoln helped Mary step from buggy, to stool, to ground, he put the stool back in the buggy while Mr. Henderson placed the suitcases on the porch. Lincoln led Mary up the five steps and to the swing. "Wait here, for me Mary, while I help Mr. Henderson with the horse and buggy." Mary swung gently back and forth, taking note of the elm trees shading the street and occasional tall oaks. The houses were mostly frame two-story houses, with porches and mature shrubs hugging the foundations. Friendly, not too different from Gibson City, but, of course, Adrian was larger.

Mr. Henderson carried the suitcases upstairs, while Lincoln, valise over his shoulder, lifted Mary in his arms and carried her across the threshold. "Welcome to our first home, Mary."

Mrs. Henderson met them at the door, wiping her hands on her apron. "Hello, Lincoln. It's good to see you again. It's lonesome in the summers. And this is Mary. It's a great pleasure to meet you, Mrs. Green. I feel as if I almost know you from Lincoln's admiring stories." She wiped her hands again, and led them up the long oak stairs. "I hope you'll like your rooms. I enjoyed gathering things together to make it as homey as I could."

At the top of the stairs, across the hall, Mrs. Henderson opened the door to the front corner room. Mary quickly surveyed the room, bright with light shining through lace curtains on two sides, a green sofa on one wall, and a fireplace, with an easy chair with ottoman, and a rocking chair nearby. Each had an afghan across the back. Hand-made, Mary surmised. There was a study corner with table, an oil lamp, chair and bookcase. Mary stepped in on the green patterned carpet and said in wonder, “Its lovely, Mrs. Henderson, so much more than I expected. We shall be very happy here.”

Smiling with pleasure, Mrs. Henderson opened the door to the adjoining room. “This is the bedroom. There’s plenty of room to put away your things.” And Mary saw that there surely was. In addition to the double bed, covered with a lovely, hand-made quilt, there was a maple dresser with another oil lamp, and a chest, two straight chairs, a bedside table, and a low stand on which was one of their trunks. Their other trunk was in the large closet, and their suitcases by the bed. The double window had draperies instead of lace curtains.

“It’s perfect, Mrs. Henderson. Thank you for making our first home so special.” Mary was almost overwhelmed. She had expected a sparse rooming house.

“I’m so glad you like it. Excuse me. I have to go down and finish dinner. It’ll be about ten minutes. I ring a bell, Mrs. Green.” She hurried down the stairs.

After one big hug and kiss, Lincoln lifted the suitcases onto the bed, opened both of them and asked, “Mary, do you want to use the dresser or the chest? We have time to unpack before dinner.” Mary pointed to the dresser, and before the bell rang, all their clothes were neatly put away.

When the bell rang, Mary took a quick look in the mirror, smoothed her hair, and headed down the stairs with Lincoln. As they passed from the hall into the dining room, Mary glimpsed a piano in the living room. Not many homes had pianos! Maybe—.

A young man rose from his seat as they entered the dining room. Lincoln embraced him saying, “Harold! So glad to see you. I did get Mary to say ‘yes’, and here she is. Mary, this is my friend Harold

Johnson. He's a divinity student, too."

"I'm happy to meet you. Lincoln has told me about you. Friends are special." Mary sat in the chair Lincoln held for her next to Mrs. Henderson. Mr. Henderson was at the foot of the table, an empty chair next to him.

"Andrew McNickelson will be in this afternoon. He's a freshman in pre-law from Chicago."

Lincoln and Harold had a lot to share as they ate their roast beef, mash potatoes, and peas, with a tomato salad. Mary noticed Harold's neatly combed brown hair, hazel eyes in an oval, clean shaven face. His face changed to match his animated conversation from smile to questioning, pressed lips to laughter. She complimented Mrs. Henderson on the food and again praised her efforts to make their rooms so nice. Then, a bit hesitantly, she asked, "I noticed you have a piano. Do you play? I enjoy music."

"A little. Mr. Henderson is the pianist, but he doesn't play much anymore. I miss it." She asked Mary, "Do you play? "

"No, but I wish I could. Music lifts the heart. I enjoy things that add beauty to life. I can see you do too from your afghans and quilt."

Mrs. Henderson smiled at the compliment. "I do enjoy sewing. I don't have much time in winter, but summers and holidays give me free time." After a few moments, she added, "Would you really like to learn to play the piano? You could take lessons at the college, and practice here when the boys are in class."

"I've never thought of that. It might help Lincoln for me to be able to play hymns, if no one else could do it. Maybe." Mary was excited at the idea, but not sure. She would ask Lincoln about it.

"That old piano is lonesome. I'd like to hear scales and beginning notes again. My Jacob took lessons." Mrs. Henderson was lost in memories, but unexpectedly spoke out, "Edward, would you please play for us a little this evening?"

Mr. Henderson looked up, surprised. He looked at his calloused hands. "I don't know whether these old hands can move well enough any more, but I'll try if you want."

Mary was wondering if she really could make music some day when she heard Harold ask, "Mary, are you planning to take classes, too?"

"Yes, Harold. I love to learn, and I wouldn't have anything to do sitting here while Lincoln is in class and studying."

"I registered this morning, and I've just been telling Lincoln that Professor Jamison's Homily class is filling up fast. He'd better register soon if he wants to get in it. I brought copies of the class offerings for Lincoln and Andrew. You can look one over and decide what classes you want." Harold handed the papers to Mary and Lincoln.

"How thoughtful of you, Harold. Thank you. We'll look it over and register right away." After dinner, Lincoln and Mary studied the offerings. Mary found a class in beginning piano, and tentatively asked Lincoln, "Do you think it would be a good idea for me to take a course in piano? Mrs. Henderson suggested it, and said it would be all right for me to practice when you and the others were in classes."

"Piano? That's a wonderful idea! You'd be good at making music, Mary."

Lincoln's enthusiasm settled it. Mary listed "Beginning Piano," added a Bible Survey course, and, after studying the science and English courses, decided to take Geology. Three classes would be enough. It was even better, for she could get all three on Monday, Wednesday, and Friday mornings.

Lincoln had no trouble deciding on his second-year seminary

classes. He had more scattered hours, but he and Mary could walk to classes together three times a week.

As they walked the four blocks to the campus under the elm trees, Mary reminisced how she and Lucy had gathered pretty pebbles in the slough that wandered through their meadow. "Lincoln, Geology will be interesting. I made a collection of jewel-like rocks from the stream we played in, really pretty transparent ones, and Mother identified some of them as jasper. Lucy's collection was just ordinary rocks. Maybe some day I can identify rocks for our children."

Lincoln did get into Professor Jamison's Homily class—just barely. Mary's Bible Survey was at 8 a.m., Piano at nine, and Geology at eleven. She would have an hour to study in the library, and walk home with Lincoln for dinner. If all the students were in class, she would have time to practice every afternoon. After buying their textbooks at the college store, choosing the second-hand ones, Lincoln made sure she knew the location of each class.

Andrew McNichelson was in the chair beside Mr. Henderson at supper that night. He was a delight with his Irish accent and stories of life in a Chicago Tenement. He would make a good lawyer, Mary thought, and his stories added welcome laughter to their table.

After supper, Mr. Henderson agreed to play the piano for them. He looked at his fingers and rubbed them before he took music out of the piano bench, selected several sheets, and began, a little hesitantly, to play "Fur Elise." After a few moments of playing, he gained confidence. It was lovely, Mary thought. He continued with a little Mozart, and then said, "I'm a little rusty, but I did enjoy playing for you." It was almost like a family gathering.

More Learning at Adrian College

Saturday, they emptied their trunks, and Lincoln and Mary walked around downtown Adrian. There were quite a few small stores, a restaurant, a bar, and a hotel. There was also a little park with a pond. Maybe on nice days they could have a picnic.

Sunday morning, Lincoln and Mary walked to the Brethren Church where Lincoln had made many friends the year before. The college Sunday School class welcomed Mary with enthusiasm. During a social time between Sunday School and the church service, Lincoln introduced Mary to Reverend Thompson, almost as tall as Lincoln, dressed simply in a business suit. Mary noticed how relaxed and casually the two talked together, as friends more than pastor and church attendee. Lincoln, evidently, was active in this church. Mary wondered what her part would be.

"Everybody seems to know you, Lincoln. You must have participated in everything last year." Mary remembered going to church with her brother Leslie when she was in Yellow Springs. They had enjoyed their youth group, but she was older now, and married.

"Sunday School and choir, and sometimes I went to the Sunday night services, because I missed you so much on Sundays. I attended the Saturday night youth group sometimes, but most of the time I had to study. This year, I don't want to do anything without you." Lincoln took Mary's hand adding, "It's time for church, come. You'll like Reverend Thompson's sermon."

As they stood to sing "Holy, Holy, Holy," Mary understood why he sang in the choir. Her voice was clear and on pitch, but just ordinary. His tenor was from deep in his throat, clear and mellow. When the choir rose to sing, she noted how few men there were in proportion to the women, and especially so few tenors.

Reverend Thompson did not stand behind the pulpit to give his sermon, but came down to the congregation, speaking intimately, as if to each one individually. His topic was, "Being a Christian." Mary was interested in his very start. He talked of the name of God, Jehovah, meaning "I am that I am," the very essence of being. Likewise, a Christian is a new creature, alive spiritually as well as physically, existent, a new being. Using frequent scriptures, he pointed out that a Christian is known for what he is, spirit, mind, and body, shown by what he does and says. And just as much for what he is not, what he will not do, and what he does not say. That was food for thought, a challenging standard, Mary thought. Did thoughts matter, too?

Early Monday morning classes began. All four of the students walked, comparing schedules and anticipations. Harold would be in most of the same classes as Lincoln, but Andy's classes were as diverse as Mary's.

Mary found she would have to memorize quite a few facts in her Bible Survey class, probably useful things to know. Geology would be easy and interesting. She was surprised that her piano lessons included basic teaching about writing music as well as reading it. She was assigned a few finger exercises and scales to practice.

In this last year of seminary, Lincoln warned Mary there would be more studying and papers required.

After the first few weeks, they developed a routine: classes, fellowship at meals, an enjoyable half hour evenings with Mr. Henderson who really enjoying playing for them, his fingers getting nimble again with practice. But evenings and spare time between classes were dedicated to study. Mary had time to practice and read books from the library, in addition to her home work. Occasionally, Mrs. Henderson would join her as she practiced in the living room, and play scales with her, octaves apart, and as Mary improved, playing the base or treble in the song she practiced, laughing together at false notes.

Weekends always included a walk if the weather permitted, and Mary encouraged Lincoln to join the choir again, offering to volunteer if she were accepted. Her voice was not exceptional, but it was an acceptable alto. Mary found the piano class helped her read the choir music. Lincoln's tenor voice really filled a gap. He also was asked to sing solo parts.

The adult Sunday School class augmented her Bible survey course. Her geology class was easiest, and most interesting. Her grandfather was right. She was now enjoying the best of all choices, except she did miss her flowers.

Two weeks before Thanksgiving, Lincoln seemed especially busy. He turned to her from his study and asked, "Mary, would you mind terribly staying here for the Thanksgiving holiday? I hate to suggest that, but I have a term paper due the first week in December, and it isn't going very well."

He did look tired, Mary thought, and maybe worried. "I can be thankful here just as well as there, and this is our home now. Just being with you is enough." Then she added, "Could I help? Maybe I could check references or organize your note cards." She wondered, though, if Mrs. Henderson would mind. She probably looked forward to the holiday without the students.

While Lincoln resumed his studies, Mary went downstairs to talk with Mrs. Henderson in the kitchen. Mrs. Henderson said she and her husband were planning to visit her sister for Thanksgiving, but they would be welcome to stay there. She added, "You've been helping me with the dishes, so you know where everything is in the kitchen. If you want to, you can cook your meals here." That would make it a special holiday, Mary thought, as she thanked her.

It was a strange Thanksgiving. Lincoln worked day and night, getting too little sleep. He was coughing at night, trying to muffle the sound so Mary wouldn't notice. He took Mary to the restaurant for Thanksgiving dinner after church, but hurried back to his books and papers.

He did finish in time to hand the paper in on Monday, but the cough persisted.

When Hendersons returned, Mary asked Mrs. Henderson if she knew of any natural remedy for a cough. Grandmother Atwood had always seemed to have something to help when they had colds or other little illnesses.

Sure enough, Mrs. Henderson had an answer. "I've noticed that cough, too, Mary. My mother used to make something she called 'honion syrup' that seemed to help us. It wouldn't hurt to try it. Why don't you help me make it so you could learn how?"

They chopped six onions into tiny pieces. Then Mrs. Henderson poured a cup of honey into the top pan of a double boiler, water in the bottom pan. She put the chopped onions into the syrup. "This has to simmer for two hours. Then we'll strain it, and put it into a jar. You can give Lincoln one warm tablespoonful every couple of hours." The "honion syrup" did seem to help a little, and in addition to a little more sleep, the coughing was almost gone.

The few weeks before the Christmas vacation sped by. Then, on December 21, Mary and Lincoln were back in Gibson City. They went first to Grandmother Atwood's home, where Mary Esther had lived since she was nine years old. Lincoln was now one of the family, sharing seminary memories with Julius, accepting Artemissa as "Mother," enjoying her company and meals. His brother Wilbert was there almost each evening visiting Lucy. There was no snow for Christmas, but all the younger children, Stephen—eleven, Grace—nine, and Artie—six, found games to entice Lincoln. He remembered the work he did with his younger brothers and sisters when they were building his family house, and the games he and Melissa invented for them to play. Wilbert joined Lincoln, Mary, and Lucy for church on Christmas Eve and again the next morning. It was wonderful being with old friends.

Of course, Mary had to visit her grandfather Julius and grandmother Roxanne Cranston. She just had to let him know how right he had been to reassure her in the time of her uncertainty. Somehow, she had found all the answers in the joy of helping Mr. Davis with the garden section, more learning, and especially, the love of Lincoln and joy of being his wife. Her grandfather hesitated a moment, and then asked, "How's Lincoln's cough?"

Mary had to admit, "He had a bad spell during Thanksgiving holiday when he was working day and night on a term paper. Mrs. Henderson made a family remedy, 'honion syrup,' that helped, and when he stopped the late night studies, he got better. He doesn't cough very much now, but once in a while."

The last few days of the Christmas vacation they spent with Lincoln's family. His mother Augusta was limping. "A little. Rheumatism," she explained. "It's kept me from my garden all fall. But it's getting better. I'll be fine when the weather gets warm." She was still interested in hearing all about Mary's studies and their life at Adrian. Mary didn't tell her of Lincoln's cough, but his mother heard him at night.

Mary pondered her comment about her garden. Who had gathered the root crops, if Augusta had been unable to do it? She took a walk in Augusta's vegetable garden. No sign of digging up the potatoes. Without telling anyone, she found a shovel and dug up a hill of potatoes, still in the ground. She set about digging up all the root crops, finding carrots, turnips, and onions. Lincoln found her, and took over the digging, while she found baskets to fill. They put most of the crop into the root cellar, taking a few samplings into the kitchen to show Augusta that her crop had been gathered and stored.

Lincoln's older brother Herbert and his family came from his farm near-by for the dinner, delicious with the found vegetables. Brother John, who was helping Lincoln's father David farm his land and Lincoln's 50 acres, and Herbert, gave Lincoln a tour of the farms, discussing spring plantings. Lincoln commented to Mary that evening, "It was so natural to be walking through those familiar fields that I helped farm for so many years. They are good memories. And I enjoyed digging the vegetables, too. Farming keeps one close to God. So many of Jesus' stories are about farming. I can use this experience in my sermons."

A Sudden Change of Plans

After the Christmas vacation, back in Adrian, it was time for final examinations. Lincoln started the late nights of studying again, and in two days the coughing was worse. Mary made more of the 'honion syrup' but it didn't seem to help this time. Mary's examinations were early, and the third day, after a night of rasping coughing, Mary said, "Lincoln, you must stay home and rest. That cough is serious."

"I can't, Mary. If I miss the examination, I will lose the entire credit, and won't graduate in June." Lincoln put on his coat and hat, and Mary wrapped the scarf around his neck. She grabbed her coat and the syrup, and insisted on accompanying him, and waiting until he finished to walk home with him.

"How was it, Lincoln? Could you control the cough enough to write the exam?" Mary gave him some more syrup.

"I did cough a lot, but muffled it pretty well with my handkerchief. I think I passed the exam, but no A." Lincoln was still coughing as they walked back to their rooms.

"Lincoln, you must rest. That cough is serious. It sounds as if comes from deep in your chest. The syrup isn't enough." Mary was now even more concerned.

"I'll rest this afternoon, Mary, but I have my last two exams tomorrow. I'll have to study some." Lincoln had his priorities, and Mary had to accept it. He did study late that night, and coughed all night, getting little sleep, but he could not be persuaded to stay home from the last two examinations.

Again, Mary walked with him and waited, checking with him between the two examinations. He was looking tired, and coughing with a rasping sound, but he would not be dissuaded from finishing his course. He leaned on Mary as they walked home, and willingly lay down as soon as they got to their rooms. Mary brought him a tray with his dinner, but he did not eat anything.

Mary asked Mrs. Henderson if she could recommend a doctor. "It's about time, Mary. I'll send Edward to fetch Dr. Murphy. I heard him coughing all night."

Dr. Murphy came in his own buggy, and hurried up the stairs with his little black bag. "How long has he had this cough, Mrs. Green?"

"Just four days this time. He had a bad spell Thanksgiving, too, and sometimes a little coughing for the last two or three years." Mary thought as she related the facts, that it was a bad pattern.

Dr. Murphy asked her to help Lincoln sit up in bed as he listened to sounds in his chest, back and front. He then carefully examined Lincoln's eyes, ears, nose, mouth, and throat. He helped Lincoln lie back down, covered him, and motioned Mary to go into the other room. He closed the door, and said, "Mrs. Green, your husband is very seriously ill. His lungs are so congested I don't see how he can breathe at all. He needs to be in a hospital."

Mary answered, "I was afraid of that. He is so strong willed, insisted on taking all his exams." Mary then asked, "Is there a hospital in Adrian?"

"Fortunately, yes. It's small, but gives good care. The fastest way to get him there is for me to take him in my buggy. I'll get his wraps on and get him ready while you pack a bag of his necessities." He noticed Mrs. Henderson with Mary, worried and ready to help. "Mrs. Henderson, is your husband here? Could he help me get Mr. Green into my buggy? Mrs. Green, you come along to help hold him in a sitting position to help him breathe." He added to Mr. Henderson, "You come along to take Mary home.

After Lincoln was settled in his hospital bed, Dr. Murphy said to Mary, "Mrs. Green, you go home with the Hendersons and rest. We're going to give him a sedative so he'll sleep, and you need to rest to be strong. It's not going to be easy. You come in tomorrow afternoon."

Reluctantly, Mary did go home. She hadn't realized how tired she was. And she did sleep. Lincoln was in good hands. Early the next morning as she read her Bible and prayed for Lincoln's healing, she decided to look through the concordance to find healing scriptures. She remembered from her survey class that Jehovah Jireh meant, The Lord who provides, and there were many healings in the Bible.

Psalm 103:3 was encouraging: "Bless the Lord O my soul; and all that is within me bless His holy name...who forgiveth all thy iniquities, and healeth all thy diseases."

She hunted more. and found in James 5:14-16, "Is any among you sick? Let him call for the elders of the church, and let them pray over him, anointing him with oil in the name of the Lord. And the prayer of faith shall save the sick, and the Lord will raise Him up; and if he have committed sins, they shall be forgiven him, that he may be healed. The effectual, fervent prayer of a righteous man availeth much."

Mary wrote these verses down, folded the paper and placed it in her pocket. She was not a "righteous man," but she was a Christian who tried to be righteous. She was not an elder of the church. Should she ask Reverend Thompson to pray for him?

She went back to the Bible. In all the Gospels, she found Jesus giving to his disciples the power to heal the sick. Was she a disciple? Then she found Mark 16:15-18 which stated that Jesus gave the power of healing to all believers, saying, "Go ye into all the world and preach the gospel to every creature. and these signs shall follow them that believe." Mary was a believer, but she had never cast out devils or spoken with new tongues, nor taken up serpents—but she could, maybe "lay hands on the sick, and they shall recover." She copied those verses, too and put the paper in her pocket with the others.

At dinner that day, with Lincoln's empty seat a haunting reminder, Harold asked Mary, "Would you mind if I went with you to visit Lincoln?"

Mary welcomed the support his presence would add. She wondered if their classes taught the laying on of hands. "I would appreciate having you with me, and I know Lincoln will be glad to see you."

Mrs. Henderson offered, "Mr. Henderson will drive you two, Mary, and I'd like to come along, too, just for a few moments."

"Lincoln would like that, Mrs. Henderson. Friends add strength to the sick. I hope he's better." Maybe he would still be sedated, and not be aware of any of them, Mary thought.

On the way to the Hospital Mary sat by Harold and gathered courage to ask him, "Have you ever prayed for the sick, Harold, and laid hands on anyone in prayer?"

"No, Mary, but I know that is taught in the Bible."

"Yes, in Mark. Here, read it." Mary handed him her copied Scripture. "It says that believers have that power, doesn't it?"

"It does, Mary. That's an awesome power. I'm just a student but

I am a believer. Do you think I could?"

"Harold, let's put our faith together and try."

Lincoln was awake, but not very alert. He seemed very glad to see them all. After the Hendersons left, promising to return to bring them home in a couple of hours, Harold and Mary chatted with Lincoln for a while, and then Mary asked if they could pray for him. Lincoln assented, and they both lay their hands on him while Harold prayed in faith for Lincoln's healing.

Lincoln, too added his faith, "Thank you, Lord, for healing me."

Mary wrote letters to both their families telling of the illness, but adding her hope for his recovery. There was a little improvement in the next few days, and by the end of a week, the cough was only intermittent. Dr. Murphy took Mary aside.

"Mrs. Green, your husband is well enough to leave the hospital, but his lungs are so damaged that he will not be able to continue his studies. He needs to be out in the open air instead of studying and working on sermons. If he continues in school and tries to minister in a church, the cough will just get worse, and he will not live long. Working in the good clean air may even heal those lungs."

Mary pondered his words, letting them sink into her heart. "Dr. Murphy, have you told him? He believes he has a call from God to preach." Lincoln had such a strong will, Mary did not know how he would take this news.

"I wanted you to know first. Let's go together to tell him." Dr. Murphy walked toward Lincoln's room.

Mary told him, as they walked, "Lincoln has been farming for years, and although he will be disappointed, I believe he will accept the truth, and return to farming. He owns 50 acres."

When Lincoln heard that because of his lungs he must give up his studies and career as a minister, he was silent for a long moment, and then he said, "When one door is shut, then I can serve the Lord wherever he chooses me to be. Farming is a useful and honorable career."

Mary gave Lincoln a kiss, and said to Dr. Murphy, "Could he stay here until tomorrow? I can pack our things and make arrangements for the train ride back to Gibson City. Will he be well enough to travel tomorrow?" Then she said to Lincoln, "Let's go back home and begin our new work on your farm together." Then she whispered to him, "We might be beginning a family, too."

Dr, Murphy said, "It's a hard trip, but he can make it. I'll give you some instructions when you pick him up tomorrow." Then he turned to Lincoln, "You're a strong man, Mr. Green. It's winter. If you rest enough, and spend a lot of time outside without working too hard, you will probably have no trouble planting your fields in the spring. The prognosis is pretty good if you work outside."

The hospital bill and Dr. Murphy's charge almost emptied their savings, but the rooms had been paid for in advance, and there was enough for the train tickets and a little to spare. As Mary packed the trunks and suitcases, she picked up her school books. It had been a good semester but it was over. Mary took her pen and wrote on the back page of her Geology book, "As my life yarn spins against other yarns, it catches the fibers, and twists into my very heart." So far? She thought. Yes, I said coolly, for the time being. She slipped the book in the trunk and finished her packing.

The Hendersons helped her send off the trunks and get her tickets. It was with great sadness that the Hendersons and Mary picked up Lincoln. They all said their goodbyes. As the train pulled out, with a sigh, Mary put her arm around Lincoln, straightened her back, and began their new life with hope and courage.

Home in a Schoolhouse

Mary Esther had not had time to notify anyone of their return to Gibson City. They went into the station, Lincoln still coughing some, but better. "Lincoln," Mary asked, "Where would you rather stay until we can find a home of our own?"

"Maybe with my parents. I could help Dad with the farm, and be close to my 50 acres." Lincoln added, "I hate to be a burden, but I can't work much right now."

"Lincoln, don't worry about that. I know your parents, and mine. They wouldn't want us to be anywhere else."

Mary pondered how to get to the farm. She could hire a buggy at the stable, or—Mr. Davis! His store was almost across the street. "Wait here, Lincoln. I'm going to find a ride."

Mr. Davis looked up in answer to Mary's voice, "Mary Esther Green! What a surprise! I thought you were in Adrian."

"We were, Mr. Davis, but Lincoln got sick—that cough, you know—and the doctor told him he had to find a career out in the open air. No more school or ministry. We came back here until we can make plans. No one knows we're here. I wrote them notes, but I'm sure they haven't arrived yet I was wondering—."

Mr. Davis interrupted, "Of course, I'll take you. Where? To your family or Lincoln's?"

"To the Green farm. God bless you, Mr. Davis." Mary waited while Mr. Davis asked his clerk to take over, and got his buggy. Gibson City was home, full of friends.

David and Augusta Green came outside as soon as they saw the buggy approaching. Before they could recover from their amazement seeing Lincoln and Mary in the buggy, Lincoln explained, "Mother, Dad, I got sick, and the doctor told me I must quit school and get outside in the fresh air. We'll find a place soon, but I didn't know where else to go right now."

"Son, this is your home! Of course, this is the place to be. Your old room is waiting for you." David Green helped Mary from the buggy, and reached to help Lincoln. "Is it that cough, Lincoln? Your mother and I have been concerned about that for years."

"Yes, Dad, my lungs are congested, in bad shape. But a little while in this fresh farm air will make a big difference." Lincoln laughed a little, and added, "I guess I was meant to be a farmer like you."

Augusta hugged Mary. "Welcome. You knew that if my son were sick, I would want him here." Augusta thanked Mr. Davis and asked him in, but he explained that he had to get back to his store.

The doctor was right. At first Lincoln sat bundled up in the winter sun, but as he improved he joined in the farm work. He planned the crops he wanted to plant on his 50 acres, and talked about building a house. His brother Herbert, visiting from his farm nearby, was discussing with Lincoln his plans for the future. Lincoln didn't like to talk about it, but the hospital and doctor bills had made a hole in their savings. Herbert casually reminded Lincoln that there was an abandoned one-room school house on his farm, saying, "It's not a real house, Lincoln, but it could be a temporary home for you and Mary while you make plans. It's not far from your 50 acres."

"Herbert, that might be a possibility. We don't want to be a burden on Mom and Dad any longer than necessary. I am feeling better." Lincoln's heart lightened. "Let's look at it, Herbert."

The old schoolhouse wasn't in good repair, but the frame was solid. There was a pot-belly stove in the middle, a cloak room on one end. The windows were dirty, but still in good shape. Outside were two outhouses, one for boys, one for girls, and a well with a rope and pulley. The bucket was missing. The roof had a few loose shingles, but there was no sign of leaking. Lincoln paced off the size. It was about twenty-five by forty feet, a rather small school, but plenty of room for two to live in.

The next day Lincoln took Mary to see the schoolhouse, and get her opinion. In her mind, she imagined dividing it into rooms, maybe a kitchen in the cloak room—except there was no window there. No, there would have to be a window in the kitchen. There could be a bedroom beside a kitchen on the end near the cloakroom, and a living room with a dining table in the other end. "Is the stove working," she asked, "and good water in the well?" It could be made into an acceptable home. She wondered about a place to keep a horse for transportation.

Yes, the stove worked, and the well had good water. She gave her approval. In February, work on the farms lessened, and the men had time to get the schoolhouse in order. Mary helped by washing the windows inside and out, cleaning trash from the cloakroom, and washing woodwork and floors. She also drew plans for dividing the space into three small rooms. The one door led into the kitchen. Mary asked if the men could make another door into the living room.

Lincoln, now much better, said with a flourish, "Your wish is my command, Madam."

As a surprise, Augusta planned with Artemissa and Roxanne to gather excess furniture from their homes to furnish the house. Grandfather Cranston invited Mary and Lincoln for dinner one Saturday in March, and the next day, when they went to work on the schoolhouse, they found it completely furnished, with a fire in the stove heating the new home.

Lincoln dug and cultivated a garden plot for Mary behind the new home, and small garden spots by the front door. By this time, Mary had shared with Lincoln that she was pregnant, baby expected in August. She did not let that stop her from planting the vegetable garden and flowers.

Augusta and David came by to take them to church on Sundays, and on warmer days in April, Lincoln and Mary borrowed their buggy for picnics in their favorite places. Farming was agreeing with Lincoln.

Early in June, Lincoln received a letter from Harold. He would soon graduate, be ordained—Reverend Johnson. He wanted to visit Lincoln and Mary before he began his new church assignment. Lincoln wrote back immediately, delighted to have a chance to be with his friend again. Augusta offered his room for the guest, happy to meet her son's friend.

It was a happy three days. Lincoln showed off his schoolhouse home, with a dinner cooked by Mary. Harold found time to comment to Mary, "It seemed our prayers for healing were not answered, since Lincoln had to give up his seminary plans.

Mary answered, "God answers in His own ways, Harold. Maybe God wanted Lincoln to be a farmer, not a preacher. He can serve God here, too, and work in the fresh air seems to have cured his cough." She offered him more pie, and added, "Don't give up praying for healings, Harold. God keeps His promises."

Lincoln got his 50 acres planted, built a little stable in half of the cloakroom to house a horse. They had their own transportation, and no longer had to borrow a horse and buggy from his father. As the weather got warmer, they delighted in having picnics on Sunday afternoons again. Lincoln was protective of Mary as the baby in her grew larger. On August 20, 1891, Roy Ezra Green was born in the schoolhouse home, his middle name taken from the Reverend Ezra Fox who had married Lincoln and Mary.

Photograph by Kevin Green

Rose Haven barn. Note Name and Date on Barn.
Photo taken in 2010.

Part III

Rose Haven Farm

Looking for Land

The summer of 1891 was busy, with Mary Esther taking care of house, garden, and baby Roy Ezra Green, while Lincoln tended his crops, and helped and enjoyed his family. But the 50 acres was too small to provide for a family. As they were spending an evening with Wilbert and Lucy, Wilbert tentatively asked Lincoln, "Would you consider buying a farm with me? I've finished college, and want to start farming, and we could combine your experience with what I've learned at college."

That started a four-way discussion. Wilbert had already asked Lucy to marry him when he was established enough to provide a home for her. The four had many shared times together and, of course, shared families. Although Lincoln was feeling very well, with no coughing since early spring, he thought it might be wise to have a partner in case he did get sick again. They talked of possibilities and problems, hopes and dreams, and in early September, Lincoln sold his

50 acres to his father, and he and Wilbert took the train to Ford County to find land to buy together.

They found a real estate agent, George Fuller, but with careful searching they found no land available to buy. Mr. Fuller suggested, "Perhaps we could look in Vermillion County, near Danville, Illinois. My father and Senator Conner own land there and they would be willing to sell." The three men took the train to Oakwood, Illinois. As they approached Danville, Lincoln was sure they were on "a wild goose chase." All they saw was woods and water. But about three miles east of Oakwood, Illinois, they found rolling prairie.

From Oakwood, they went west and a little north by buggy to the land Mr. Fuller's father and State Senator Conner were willing to sell. It was 240 acres, on the west side of the road, at a price of $52.50 an acre. They decided to buy it. There was an old 4-room house, uninhabitable, on the south part. As they paced the land, Lincoln divided it into two parts of 120 acres each.

The south half was pasture and unbroken prairie. The north part had been planted with corn for many years. They decided the south part was more valuable, and would cost $55 an acre, and the north part $50. He gave Wilbert the choice. Wilbert chose the north portion.

Back in Gibson City, Lincoln described the farm to Mary, "It's black prairie soil on gently rolling land planted in corn. There's a low corner in the north with a little standing water and a big Cottonwood tree. Wilbert and I thought that would be a good place to build a house."

"That sounds like a wonderful farm," Mary said, "but there isn't a house on it. How long will it take to build a place for us to live?"

"There's a little 4-room-house on the north half, that Wilbert chose, but it's not in good enough condition to live in. Wilbert and I can build a house before Christmas. You and Roy can stay here until we finish it. I'll make a good place for us, Mary," Lincoln promised.

"Be sure it's large enough for a family, Lincoln. This schoolhouse is fine now—" Lincoln laughed, and asked, "How many rooms do you want, Mary?"

"How many children do you want, Lincoln? We don't want to raise Roy all by himself, do we?" Mary laughed, too. "Let's build a home that will last for three generations!"

While the men were looking for a farm, Mary busied herself watching Roy Ezra and harvesting her vegetable garden. She would have to can enough to keep them until her garden in Vermillion County grew. As she worked in the garden, she sometimes brought the baby and lay him on a blanket near her. One day he started to cry. She found a bug crawling across his face. She flicked the bug away and picked him up. The ground was not safe for her baby. A basket would not stop a bug, either. Then her face brightened. Putting Roy safely in his crib, she went to the cloak-room barn and found the wheelbarrow. She scrubbed it clean, dried it with a rag, and put in a pillow, then Roy in his blanket. She wheeled him out to the garden to pick and store her crop beside him in the wheel barrel, repeating happily to herself, "Make it do, use it up, wear it out, or do without." She had a lot of produce to can, and after the cans had cooled and seals had been checked, she packed them carefully into bushel baskets for the move.

The two brothers worked hard that fall building a two story house on the land near the place where the two halves came together, just north of the pond and the big cottonwood tree, The ground was a little lower and flatter than the rolling prairie. They planned a house of seven rooms, four on the first floor, and three upstairs, plus a large storage room. The front faced the road, but not too close. A front door led into a living room, and from a small front hall, stairs rose to the second floor, still unfinished. The little hall connected the living room to a bedroom. Behind the two front rooms was a large dining room and kitchen combination, with a little bathing room off the living room side. Lincoln bought a bath tub with a pipe for water to drain to the outside. A side door faced toward the driveway, with the pond a long stone's throw away. Lincoln had already bought a cook stove and two pot-bellied stoves, one in the living room and one in the dining area. There were grates in the ceilings for heat to rise to the upper bedrooms.

The two men had built the house in record time. They had even plastered the downstairs. Wilbert and Lincoln stood near the road admiring their accomplishment. "You're all ready to move in, Lincoln. You can go get Mary and Roy Ezra." Wilbert said.

"Not quite yet, Wilbert. We can't drink water out of that pond. Let's dig a well." So they took their shovels and started digging. They did hit good, clean water at about 20 feet.

Mary was surprised when Lincoln came back to Gibson City a week before Thanksgiving, saying, "Our home is ready, Mary Esther. We even dug a well! Let's move to our new farm."

"How could you possibly build a house that quickly, Lincoln? You two must have had a great deal of help." Mary had always known Lincoln was resourceful and capable, but this was almost beyond belief.

"The upstairs isn't finished yet. The neighbors did help with the roof raising. I remember the big party we had when neighbors came to help us put the roof on our house when I was just seven. It wasn't a party this time, but we did appreciate the help. You'll like our neighbors." Lincoln looked around the little schoolhouse. "We don't have too much furniture. Do you think we could get it all on one spring wagon?"

"We can try. Is there pasture for two more horses, Lincoln? And maybe a cow?" Mary was thinking ahead.

"I think there would be plenty of pasture. Meg was doing pretty well finding fodder."

Lincoln found a large spring wagon, and the limited furniture did fit, and the few tools he already owned. They would have to buy those he had borrowed from his father. But then Lincoln looked at a group of baskets Mary had pulled out of the cloak room area. "Do we have to fit these in, Mary? We can get baskets in Oakwood."

"Lincoln, we won't have a garden until spring and no food from it until summer. What did you think we would eat? "Mary lifted the packing from one basket, revealing jars of fruit and vegetables.

Lincoln was speechless. He put his arms around Mary, and finally found words, "Mary, what a treasure you are!"

With rearranging, Lincoln did fit the baskets into the big wagon. They made quick visits to say goodbye to their families, and set out for the long drive from Gibson City to Oakwood, Mary fitting Roy Ezra, warmly wrapped, into a basket bed between them. At Mary's feet was a basket of food her mother had packed for the trip. Father David Green had even provided food for the horses on the trip.

On Thanksgiving Day 1891, Lincoln, Mary, and Roy Ezra moved into the house. Their urgent task now was to finish the barn for the animals in the barnyard just west of the house. They made a trench to take water from the well to the trough just past the fence. All along, Wilbert, in addition to helping Lincoln, was working on the abandoned house on his farm. Wilbert and Lucy were planning to marry in December. Mary insisted he stay with them in their warm house during his double carpentry efforts. They had gleaned a little corn from the fields, augmenting the dry grass and corn stalks for the animals. Mary ground a supply, too, for making corn bread along with the flour and other necessities they purchased. The jars of vegetables and fruit were welcome. They did get a cow for milk, and a few chickens to provide eggs and some meat.

When Lincoln took Mary to the United Brethren Church near Oakwood, she found he already had a circle of friends in the Sunday school class. And, yes, Lincoln was singing in the choir. Mary decided to sit with Roy Ezra and listen instead of placing him in the cradle class. Lincoln's coughing had not returned. Their life was settling into a winter routine when, on December 22, Wilbert persuaded them to accompany him to Gibson City to stand up with him and Lucy at their wedding. Lincoln found Josh, the teen-age son of their neighbor to tend the animals.

Back in the familiar room she and Lucy had shared, Mary now admired the lovely royal blue dress Lucy had chosen for her wedding dress. It brought out the lovely blue of her eyes and accented the blond curls. Lucy was even more beautiful than usual. Mary wondered if her dear grandmother Atwood would have another treasure to give her third granddaughter as a wedding gift. She was wearing her treasured broach. Sure enough, her grandmother came in to admire the bride and fastened a string of pearls around her neck. "My husband had these imported from the Far East. Your dress was made for this accent, Lucy. Wear them often, and may my love go with you."

This wedding was in the church—more formal. Their house was too small for the many friends and relatives whom they wanted to invite. Mary and Lincoln enjoyed proudly presenting their baby and greeting their many friends and family members after the ceremony and at the reception. Mary wondered how long it would take for them to find new friends in their new home. Life was full of changes and challenges, but she had her loving family in her heart with wonderful memories to add new ones to.

A Sticky Solution

Although the land on the south half was worn down by years of corn crops, Mary found land near the house and pond that had not been planted in corn. It would be her vegetable garden. But Lincoln knew that the fields would not grow good crops. Mary thought back to her Botany classes. Clover! It, if it is plowed into the soil instead of harvesting it, would enrich. the soil. "Lincoln, it would be better to wait a year to plant regular crops, and get the soil in better condition, wouldn't it?"

"Of course, Mary. It would be better in the long run, but what would we live on? My 50 acres didn't bring in enough crops to give us much money, and I used the sale price as a down payment on this farm." Lincoln wondered if he could find a job somewhere nearby.

"I still have a little money left from my teaching. Is there even a little corn in those fields? Were there any other crops on the farm, Lincoln?"

"All of the fields were planted in corn. We found a little in the north field, but it wasn't very much. Maybe there's still enough for the horses and a cow. Back of the pond over there, there's a little plot of sorghum. It seemed to be thriving, somehow."

"Do you know how to make sorghum, Lincoln?" Mary remembered the good molasses cookies her mother had made, and sorghum on pancakes. "Everybody likes sorghum!"

"My father grew some sorghum some years ago. I remember that after we harvested the canes, we had to cut them into pieces, grind and press the juice from them. We then had to boil the juice for days until it was thick enough, and sweet enough. Mother helped us put it into jars. I even remember the heavy dark stuff left in the bottom of the big kettle. It was too thick for regular use, but it did make good cookies. We called it 'Black strap molasses'." Lincoln thought a little while. "Mary, I think I could do it."

"Could we make some now?" A little sweetness would be welcome, Mary thought.

"Probably not, Mary. It's all dried up now. But it will grow again this spring, or I could even plant more. That lower ground seems to be perfect for it." Lincoln was getting an idea.

"Lincoln, would you mind if I tried something? I wonder if I cut up some of those dry stalks, and put them to soak in water, if, maybe, there's still some sweetness that would dissolve in the water, and then boil down to sorghum? A little sweet syrup would be nice to have."

Lincoln laughed. "I doubt it, Mary, but it's not time for planting yet. I can help you try."

It did make sweet syrup, edible, but not special. "Next year I'll make you gallons, Mary. It will probably be the only usable crop." Lincoln was thinking of the fields of clover that would have to be plowed under to enrich the land. No crops to harvest and sell this year. He put his head in his hands, discouraged. "Mary, farming is a waiting game. We have to wait for crops to grow to pay that mortgage due in September, and this farm won't grow anything this year except sorghum. What kind of farm grows only a little field of sorghum? Maybe we should have rented instead of buying a farm so soon."

"You're just tired, Lincoln." Mary laid her hand on Lincoln's shoulder, "Let's think of ways we could earn ready cash. We're young and strong, and God has given us minds to think with and hands to work with."

"Of course, Mary. How could I forget?" Lincoln took Mary's hand, bowed his head, and prayed, "Dear Father, how great and merciful you are! We praise and worship You. We praise you and thank you for all the blessings you have given us. We are Your children, and You have promised to meet all our needs according to your riches in heaven. We lift up to you our need for cash for our needs and to pay the mortgage on the farm in September. Show us your plan for us to meet this need. Amen."

Mary thought of her mother's slogan, "Make it do, wear it our, use it up." Lincoln, we'll have the sorghum. Let's make it do. We will have one good crop this year. We can make some sorghum."

"Yes, Mary. Let's grow more, and make a lot of sorghum and sell it. It will take a lot of effort, and many farmers don't want to take the time to grind it and boil it down. but everyone likes a little sweet once in a while. How much sorghum would it take to earn that much money and help us live, too? I had been thinking we might sell some sorghum cane. It makes good fodder. But you're right, Mary. Selling the sorghum molasses would be more profitable. We have to use what God gives us, and on this farm, this year, He has provided sorghum."

First, they went through the corn fields, gleaning the dry remnants. Lincoln cleared them, ready to plant clover in the early spring. Then he cut the sorghum cane for fodder. As soon as the ground was ready, he planted clover in all the fields. None of the neighbors had ever planted clover, and were curious to see what difference it would make in the land. Then he planted much more sorghum in the lower land. To make enough sorghum to sell, he planned carefully fashioned equipment especially for that process. He deepened the pond to make a little hill on which he built a mill house to grind and press the cane. He arranged a pipe to carry the liquid from the mill to the building he designed to hold the fire and kettle for boiling down the sorghum juice, and then he designed a packing shed near the barn.

"What can we put the sorghum molasses in to sell it, Mary?" Lincoln asked.

Mary thought. "We could order jars or little jugs from the Sears and Roebuck Catalog. But that would cost money in advance. I know, let's use my empty canning jars for the first batch, and buy more after you sell some."

The clover covered the fields, and the sorghum crop grew beautifully. Lincoln was whistling when he went out to cut the first ripe canes and place them in the mill press, and the pipe saved back-breaking carrying of loads of juice. It was not easy work, and required patience, but in late spring they had their first dozens of jars of sorghum ready to sell.

Mary helped pour the thick sorghum molasses into the jars. As they packed them into the baskets, Lincoln noticed that pasted on each one was a neat paper with the words, "Sorghum Molasses from the Lincoln H. Green Farm," and a water-color painting of a bundle of sorghum cane.

Mary watched Lincoln load the baskets into the spring wagon. He was dressed in a clean, freshly ironed shirt and overalls. How handsome he was! He planned to drive the team around the long way to town, stopping at every farmhouse to see if they wanted to buy fresh sorghum, and then go into town to ask there.

That day, while Lincoln was offering the sweet syrup for sale, Mary scraped the thick sticky "black strap" from the kettle into a big stone crock. She had to use her fingers to push the sticky stuff from the big spoon. What was this worth? Too thick to sell, she thought as she pushed the wooden lid onto the crock. Then she knew! She got out the big mixing bowl, and into it she measured flour, baking powder from her precious store, eggs, and a little cream from the top of the milk. Lincoln's mother had made cookies from it, and she could, too. She measured a cup of the sticky residue, scraped it carefully from the cup, licking her fingers after getting the last bit from the cup. It did taste good! It took a long time to stir it into the dough, but after she dropped spoonfuls on the cookie sheet, she licked the spoon. Mmm. And the cookies were as special as Lincoln remembered. Roy Ezra gave his approval by asking for more.

The moment Lincoln dragged into the house that evening after taking care of the horses, he smelled the cookies. "Mary! This takes me right back to my childhood. How did you get the recipe?" He ate four cookies before he even mentioned his long day's rounds.

"Come on, Lincoln, tell me how it went." Mary was impatient to know.

Without saying a word, Lincoln pulled out of his pockets more money that they had seen since they had paid the hospital bills and bought the land. "There—and they want more. All we can make!"

"Wait until they find out how many things they can make from this molasses. Lincoln, do we have enough canes to make enough sorghum to pay the mortgage?"

Lincoln counted the money carefully, and put aside one smaller pile. "Well, even after the tithe, there's one fourth of the money.

There's enough cane for at least five more, maybe six. Mary, we're going to make it, the good Lord willing."

That called for a hug from Mary. "Lincoln, we'll have to order jars right away. There aren't enough jars for more than one more set. And I'll need more to can the garden produce this year. Maybe jugs would work, too, for the sorghum."

After dinner and playing with Roy before putting him to bed, Lincoln looked through the Sears Roebuck Catalog. He made out a big order, enough for six more kettlefuls of sorghum juice, with cans for Mary's produce, too. It took most of the profits from the first sales.

Lincoln earned the nick-name "Sorghum Green," making and selling sorghum for several years, until the farm produced record crops. He went farther and farther, into other counties. One evening, in the second year, Mary was waiting and waiting for him to come home. She began to worry. He had never been that late before. Then, at nine p.m., she prayed: "Dear Father in Heaven, Lincoln is your child, and you know where he is, and have him in your care. I will trust in your care. Protect and watch over him." She felt a sense of peace, and went to bed and to sleep. Lincoln came home the next evening, reporting that he, too had been concerned about Mary worrying, since he had gone so far he could not get home that evening. But at nine p.m., exactly, he felt a sense of relief, confident she was also at peace. He often went on two-day selling trips after that. They made the mortgage payment early.

Original two-family house on Rose Haven Farm shared by both Lincoln and Willard's families. Family members say the side porch was added years after the main part of the house. This photo, about 1958, shows Roy with his back to the camera, and a hired man, removing a tree. Kevin and Sue's home is now on this site.

Two-Family Home

The clover crop of 1892 was plowed under, and the land ready for new crops in the spring of 1893. Wilbert's crops had been good, but the little house he had prepared so lovingly had one deficiency. He had dug a dry well, and was carrying water from the well he and Lincoln had dug at the big house.

The two families were celebrating Christmas together in Lincoln and Mary's home, watching Roy enjoy the decorated tree and the new toys his father had made for him. After dinner and the dishes were put away, Mary took Lincoln aside and asked, "Would you mind if we asked Wilbert and Lucy to live with us? We can quickly finish the upstairs. You and Wilbert bought the farm together, built this house together, and dug this well together. We are family, love each other, and could get along. I can see that Lucy is expecting, and I suspect I am, too."

"We share the barn, too. Are you sure it would not mean more work for you, Mary? I'm sure Wilbert and I would enjoy being together more. We've worked together all our lives." Lincoln and Mary discussed it a little while planning which rooms to offer and how to share tasks. Then Lincoln said to Wilbert and Lucy, "The little house is going to be a bit crowded this spring when you have your little one. Mary and I would be happy if you would join us in this house."

Mary could see the relief in her sister's face as they talked it over and decided to combine their families. Lucy confessed that she had been a little fearful of pregnancy and bearing a baby alone in the little house without water. Mary had appreciated the nearness of her family where Roy Ezra was born. The two families melded beautifully. The men tended the animals together, and sometimes helped each other with plowing and planting. Best of all, they shared their meals, and went to church together on Sundays. Lincoln, with no woods on his land, arranged with a friend in the choir to clear some of the dead wood and excess brush in his 40 acres of woods and stream in exchange for bringing home fallen logs and dead trees for fire wood. Then, one day at church, Wilbert heard Mr. Bartlett mention that he was going to dig some coal. Interested, he asked him where. Mr. Bartlett told him all about the coal available for the digging. It had once been a thriving business, but now was abandoned, and anyone who wanted to put in the labor could get himself some coal. It wasn't a mine, but right near the surface. It didn't take long for Wilbert and Lincoln to plan a trip there to dig coal for their pot-bellied stoves.

Lucy found interesting games to play with Roy when Mary was busy with her chickens or garden. Her garden was large, with lots of vegetables to can, and enough flowers to have flowers on the table through the summer, and still keep the garden beautiful, with plenty of blossoms to give away. She inspired Lucy to plant a garden, too, but mostly vegetables. In the evenings, they sewed together to make clothes for their expected babies, and each of them made a baby quilt.

When the fields were ready, Lincoln was pleased to see the dark brown of good prairie soil. He planted corn, oats, and clover in one field that seemed to need more nourishment, and plenty of sorghum cane. Wilbert had learned from Lincoln to rotate his crops, and also planted clover to enrich one field. In the evenings by lamplight, Mary made the labels for the sorghum, and she still helped fill jars, but she asked Lincoln to help her scrape the "black strap" into the crock. As he was scraping it one day, Mary asked him "The sorghum cane is good fodder, isn't it? I'm wondering if the mash left after mashing the juice from the canes would be good food for my chickens. We shouldn't waste it. 'Waste not, want not.'"

Lincoln laughed. "It would make good chicken food, or fodder. "Waste not, want not." That's a good motto, Mary."

On June 7, 1893, Wilbert rode into Oakwood to ask Dr. Murphy to come help with Lucy's giving birth. It was a girl, named Eulalie. How grateful Lucy was to have Mary's experienced help.

Three weeks later, on June 29, Alta was born—Alta means 'high' in Latin. They were two busy mothers, caring for their babies, Roy, the house, chickens, gardens, and meals.

All that spring and summer Lincoln was not only tending his crops and cutting firewood, but also making and selling sorghum. He was traveling farther to new markets, often stayed overnight. It was a good and prosperous year. In the fall, after he paid the mortgage, Lincoln asked Mary if there was anything special she wanted. She thought for a moment, then stated, "Our children will need trees to play with and for shade. I'd like several trees in the side yard. The Cottonwood tree is too far from the house for play, and the pond with the water lilies too dangerous for toddlers. And we will need an orchard."

"Mary," Lincoln said in admiration, "you are so wise, and can see future needs. How could I live without you?" Wilbert also bought trees for an orchard. Lincoln had bought larger trees for the yard. The orchard trees were all merely sticks, but they would grow. He also bought a camera for Mary, but kept it secret until Christmas.

In 1894, Lincoln and Wilbert added a pig pen and raised hogs. The crops were good, and there was plenty of corn to feed the animals and sell, in addition to wheat and oats, and the clover in rotation. Again, Lincoln made and sold the sorghum. The extra money was good to have, and he saved it to be ready for the bad seasons that would come.

With Roy and Alta in Sunday school, Mary Esther accepted leadership of the cradle class. The babies were not very much trouble in their cribs, and it was good for Roy to play and learn with other children, enjoying different toys. Then Mary, with the camera Lincoln had given her for Christmas, began taking pictures of the babies and toddlers. She improvised a dark room, and developed and printed the pictures herself. At first, she gave the pictures to the mothers, but they were so pleased that they insisted on paying her for them. Sometimes Lucy helped. The Sunday before Christmas, Lucy watched the children while Lincoln, Mary, and Wilbert went caroling in Oakwood. That Christmas, too, for the first time, Lincoln bought oranges to put in the toes of the stockings. Mary remembered the lemon seeds from the lemonade of their picnic in her special place—she had planted them, and one little lemon tree was growing tall on her kitchen window sill. She planted the orange seeds in a broken cup and a jar with a nicked top that wouldn't seal. She already had violets in the kitchen window.

With his rich tenor in the choir, and his many acquaintances and friends from church and his sales trips, Lincoln was frequently asked to sing at weddings and funerals. He enjoyed singing, and was gracious to accept, even when he was tired from his farming.

Lucy enjoyed watching the babies, and urged Mary to join the

Ladies Aid. It was pleasant to share news and anecdotes with her friends from church, and to share in the fund raising. Always innovative, she and Julie Watson devised a plan for making money-raising fun. They made aprons out of flour sacks for each lady in the group, and presented them to members with this little poem written by Mary:

For Ladies Aid

This neat little apron is sent to you
And this is what we'd wish you'd do:
The little pocket you plainly see
For a special purpose is meant to be.
Now, measure your waistline, inch by inch,
And see that your measure doesn't pinch.
For each small inch you measure around
Throw into the pocket a penny sound.
The game is fair, you will admit;
You waist your money—we pocket it.
The money you so freely pay
Is spent by us in the wisest way.

Father Green and Augusta had visited them just after Alta was born, and were so impressed with the farms in the community and eager to be nearer Lincoln and Mary that he sold his land in East Bend County and bought land north of Oakwood. John had already left to farm on his own, and Emmet also decided to settle near Oakwood. Emma had married John Carpenter, a blacksmith, and he also decided to settle in Oakwood. Now Lincoln had the best of all possible worlds—their farm and family, and now many members of their family to share picnics, walks in the woods, and special holidays.

Now over 100 years old, this yellow rose bush is part of the original stock Mary planted at Rose Haven Farm from the discarded plants Lincoln brought home to her. It continues to bloom on the property.

Dead Roots and Dry Sticks

In September, Lincoln took his hogs to Chicago to sell, and on the way home stopped at a nursery to buy a plant for Mary. As he chose a lilac bush, he noticed men loading dry rooted plants with dead-looking branches into a pile. Curious, he asked what they were piling up. "Rose bushes that didn't sell." One man said. They looked dead, but Lincoln knew Mary's skill with rooting branches that seemed dead.

"What would you charge me for those dead plants?" he asked.

"Nothing. You can have them if you'll haul them away." Without hesitation, Lincoln loaded the huge pile of discarded rose bushes into his wagon.

When Lincoln drove the wagon into their yard, Wilbert looked at the load of dry rose bushes, and said, "What on earth do you want with all those dry roots and dead sticks? We have plenty of kindling already."

Lincoln ignored his skepticism, and called Mary to look. "Mary, the manager of the nursery let me have these discarded rose bushes just for taking them away. I was sure you could find some life in them, and coax them to grow."

Mary reached into the truck and scratched one branch with her fingernail. Sure enough, there was green under the bark. "Roses! Dozens and dozens of roses! Lincoln, we'll have the most beautiful farm in Illinois." Lincoln unloaded the bushes not far from the well. He knew water was the first step.

Lucy, unexcited, said, "Mary, have you thought about how much work it will take to get those planted?"

"Don't you worry about them, Lucy. Beauty is worth the price. If you'll watch the children, I'll take care of the roses." Mary started pumping water to fill the laundry tubs. Lincoln worked beside her, handing her a pair of heavy work gloves to protect her hands from the thorns, and the two worked together putting the dry bushes into tubs, buckets, and any big container they could find. They couldn't find enough containers. Mary thought and thought, and finally said, "The pond! We can tie some loosely in bunches and put them in the pond." And they did.

It was a long, slow process. Mary trimmed each rose bush, putting the branches into the pond water to root them. So many! Where would she plant them all? She was saving the roses, giving them a haven. She would start by lining the road in front of their farm so passers-by could enjoy the beauty. Lincoln helped her put the roots in the wheel barrel and dug the holes while she planted them. There were enough to have a few at the front edges of the driveway. That took several days wedged between other duties. The twigs would have to wait until they developed roots. Mary patiently loaded buckets of water into the wheel barrel and watered the plants whenever there was not enough rain. They had to wait until spring to see the results.

She put the twigs in their water containers in the barn near the stalls so the warmth of the animals would keep them from freezing, but kept the water levels constant.

With the warm days of April, the green shoots showed above most of the roots, and that summer the bushes flourished, but there were few roses. Not all of the twigs rooted, but many of them did, and Mary planted them on both sides of the driveway, up to the front yard where the wagons and plows turned toward the barn and fields. There were enough to line her vegetable garden with roses, too, but it was not until 1896 that the roses were in full bloom. That is when the farm was named, "The Rose Haven Farm."

In spite of care of children, chickens, and home, Mary's garden was spectacular. In addition to the vegetables, she always had lots of flowers. People passing by would stop to admire the beauty, and if she saw them, she always picked a bouquet for them. In the pond, Lincoln placed fish, and Mary took care of the water Lilies, which bloomed with fragrant flowers. Mary gave them away. One of the earliest memories of Alta, then four, was watching her father draw circles with a string tied to his pencil on a big sheet of butcher paper. She asked what he was drawing, and he said, "Concentric circles to design your mother's garden for this summer." He explained further, "Con means with, and centric, center. So I'm drawing circles with a center." It was a spectacular garden.

Oakwood was growing, too. The first cabin was built in 1813, near old Indian burial grounds and the Middle Fork River. Gradually, after Salt was discovered along "Salt Creek," and coal found, at first available to anyone who wanted to dig it, was later commercialized, the town grew. The greatest help was the railroad, with the station built in 1872 on donated land. It was built quickly because of a fortunate accident. Lumber intended for Danville was unloaded in Oakwood. Before the mistake was discovered, the station was almost finished. Oakwood had been incorporated in 1870. The Christian Church was a center of activity, too, and organizations, called "Lodges," were popular. And several general stores made shopping easier.

In 1887, Mr. Longstrech traded two bushels of corn for a barber chair, and set up a black man, John Cole, in business. John didn't do so well, so Mr. Longstrech, with a comb, clippers and a pair of scissors, took over. According to the *History of Oakwood*, he got the clippers caught in a man's hair, and the clippers had to be taken apart to extricate them. He didn't charge for the haircuts while he was learning. An ambitious entrepreneur, in 1891, in addition to barbering, he was mending shoes and selling sandwiches and soft drinks. He had learned to mend shoes when he was twelve, taught by his father. In 1918, when his son came home from the Great War, they founded a restaurant, "The Blue Room."

Vermillion's first school was built in 1829, and in 1840, the Merry Posie School was built not far from Oakwood. When Michael Oakwood, having learned "his 3-Rs" wanted to study grammar, no text could be found. A friend, driving cattle to Chicago, finally bought one for him. In the 1860's the teacher, a man, asked to be relieved of his contract to teach when he learned he could earn more money selling organs. The director refused to release him. Before long the schoolhouse burned down and many thought it was not accidental. The second, and maybe the third schoolhouse, was built on the State Road, but in 1892 the classes were moved to Oakwood. That one-room school had eighty-three students, from six to twelve, with two classes going on at the same time. It was difficult. In 1894, a new school was started for the upper grades. It grew from two rooms, and two grades, to four rooms, a complete high school, and finally, in 1915 a large Township High School was built east of the State Road.

The families grew. After Roy and Alta, Esther was born March 10, 1896.

In November of 1897, Mary and Lincoln received a letter from Julius and Artemissa Cranston, urging them to come to Gibson City for Christmas. Mary thought about how much they missed Lincoln's father after his death, and said to Lincoln, "Is it too far for us to go to Gibson City for Christmas this year? It would be good for the children to know their grandparents, and it's been a long time since I've seen my parents."

Lincoln didn't answer for a long moment. "It's a long way, Mary. I know our parents went a lot farther in their covered wagons, with little children, too, but it's winter, and the weather is uncertain. Let's think about it."

Mary's heart sank a little. She wanted to see her parents again. It might be better in warmer weather, but farm work filled the spring and summer months. And her garden had to be tended.

But Lincoln had not dismissed the idea. He looked up a map in Oakwood. There were good road systems in Illinois, with every township laced with roads every square mile. He could cut across country, not go the long way around through Urbana and Champaign. He had been almost that far on his sorghum sales trips. It would be about forty miles, and they could travel about 20 miles a day, maybe a little more with a light load. If he put the side-boards up on his wagon, and piled a lot of straw in the bottom, it might not be too cold and windy for the children. And they had blankets.

At supper that night, he shared his memories of his trip as a six-year-old from Ohio to Illinois by covered wagon, and asked Mary questions about her trip by covered wagon from Ford County to West Bend Township when she was nine. He described the snow storm, shivering when he had to get out of the wagon. Being a pioneer was not easy, but there were good times, too. Then he reminded them how nice and warm it was in their home with the pot-bellied stove. After all that remembering, he asked them how they would feel about going to Grandma's house in their wagon, a long trip, maybe two days.

Mary was so proud of the way he introduced the idea to the children. Roy was six, and Alta four. They would remember the trip. Esther, just one, would not. Roy thought it would be an adventure. Alta was ready for anything Roy approved.

Lincoln made the decision. "We will take the trip, and let your mother visit her mother and father, and you will see your other grandmother and grandfather. Mary, I know how much you miss your parents. It's worth the trip to celebrate our Lord's birth with them this year." There were tears of joy in Mary's eyes.

Mary had already knitted hats, gloves, and scarves for the children, and Lincoln's were still keeping him warm. She spent her evenings making gifts for her parents, and for Stephen, Grace, and little Artie, still living at home. She had already been making new clothes for her children's Christmas. Lincoln made a little wagon for Roy, with a crudely carved horse, and Mary made cloth dolls for Alta and Esther, all dressed with coat and hat. Lucy helped, and made gifts for their parents, too, for them to take.

Mary checked the layered clothing of the children, and helped them wrap the blankets around them after they climbed into the straw-lined wagon on December 20, 1897. They loaded baskets of food, bottles of water, and feed for the horses. Mary had a large basket and blankets for Esther between her and Lincoln on the front seat, all of them warmly bundled.

The sun shone on that trip, and the Christmas visit was wonderful. Grandma Cranston had bought very special gifts for the children: For Roy, a blue metal chariot with two metal horses he could hitch and unhitch. The wheels actually turned, and the coachman held a little whip. For Alta, a doll with a cloth body but china head, hands and feet, dressed in a beautiful gown sewn by Grandma. She named the doll "Sweetheart" and lay her next to the doll her mother had made for her, saying, "Now my dolly has a sister."

With the joy of seeing her family and friends in Gibson City that Christmas, Mary wrote a little poem to send her mother:

Merry Christmas

A dear little land called Memory
I follow this time of year.
For it leads me back to other days
And friends that my heart holds dear.
"'Tis a happy trail to follow,
Old joys again are new,
As I come with a "Merry Christmas"
Down memories to you.

In 1898, the seven-room house was getting crowded, with four adults and five children. Wilbert and Lucy decided to move to the house inherited from David Green on the north edge of Oakwood. They later built a lovely Victorian house in the town of Oakwood.

In the fall of that year, Roy—seven, began attending the new one-room school in Oakwood. He had to walk about two miles down the road and then along the railroad track. Mary decided that Alta—five, who was very bright, was also ready to start school. Roy was very protective as they walked to and from school together. It was a big school, with the eighty-three students, and two teachers teaching classes at the same time. Esther and Ruth would later attended that school, and Vivian would for a year or two, but by then a middle school had been opened, so it wasn't so crowded. They received a good education there.

In October 1898 Ruth was born, and in 1900, along came a brother for Roy—Vivian Julius. And Lucy and Wilbert, after Eulalie, had Gladys, born in 1895. The farms prospered. In 1905, Lincoln's father died, and Lincoln traded his inheritance of 60 acres of his father's land north of Oakwood with Wilbert for 60 acres of Wilbert's land adjoining Lincoln's. At the same time, Lincoln bought 60 acres across the road from his farm from George Mason, enlarging his farm to 240 acres. There was a small house on that land not far from the Green farm house.

In the spring of 1900, Uncle Martin Atwood came for a visit. At a family dinner with all the relatives living in Oakwood, Martin observed that the big kitchen-dining room was really crowded. He talked to Lincoln and Mary, suggesting that if they approved, he could extend the house in the back to add another room, a kitchen, leaving the big room for a larger dining area. Mary, especially, was excited about having a new kitchen. Young and uninvolved yet, Uncle Martin set about modifying the back wall, adding a new back door as he built a narrow kitchen across the back of the house, with a window on one side, and an extra side door on the other. The sink and stove were on back of the dining room wall, and cupboards along the back wall. Mary was delighted with the additional cupboards and handy work space.

The happy, prosperous years went by quickly. To Roy, Alta, Esther, and Ruth, born in 1898, was added Vivian "Vee" Julius in

1900. When Vivian was born, Mary asked Alta to take over the care of Ruth, and all their lives, they had a very close relationship. Lincoln, still singing in the choir, was also serving as Superintendent of the Sunday School. Mary, active in the Ladies Aid society as well as in turn handling the cradle classes, was also taking pictures of the babies. Family devotions were an important part of every day life. One Oakwood resident established a newspaper, but it lasted only ten years. They also read the *Urbana Courier* once a week. Mary read a poem wondering why farmers never smiled. She couldn't resist sending in an answer, which was published:

Courier

Who ever saw a farmer smile,
Or speak in happy vein?
When one of them stops to talk awhile,
It's always too much rain
Or else it's too dad blasted dry
Or frosts will kill the crop
And he's chock full of reasons why
The market's bound to drop.
A chronic mourner is this bird
Who tills the verdant soil
His woes the year around are head,
For naught has been by Hoyle
As pessimist he takes the cake;
He thrives on sighs and moans.
For him, life's some long bellyache.
His system racked with groans

—Unknown Author, *Urbana Courier*

The Answer

It Seems that Some of 'em Smile
"Whoever sees farmer smile?"
I often have, my son,
For I have lived for quite a while
Where farming's being done.
He smiles when discontented strike
At city rents and bills,
And thanks the Lord for unlike
Where His green earth he tills.
He smiles when needed rains come down,
When hungry mouths are fed.
He smiles at corn silk turning brown,
At apples hanging red.
He smiles at gains that work no harm,
Enough! But mark it down
The smiling farmer's on the farm,
Not loafing round in town.

—Yours truly, Mary C. Green, Fithian, Ill.

The Lincoln Green family developed a custom of walking in the woods every Sunday afternoon when weather permitted, often with picnics. One of their favorite places was beside Stoney Creek, winding through a woods just off the road to Urbana. Both parents taught the children to recognize birds by sight and by their songs, and they all searched for nuts, mushrooms, and wild flowers hidden in the brush and leaves. Mary also enjoyed her Botany Club to share her interest in flowers. In 1897, the Botany Club invited Lincoln to be their speaker. Mary C. Green had written many verses about various flowers, always happy to share them with her friends. But Lincoln surprised them by sharing with them this poem he had written:

Spring Beauty

How delightfully frail thou art,
Of fairy form in every part,
By fairies over the hillside spread,
And timid, for at Nature's frown
Or clouded sky or hidden sun,
Thou bendest low thy head.
Yet blessed message dost thou bring,
Thou beauty of the early spring,
The gem of hill and mead.
Thou speakest of a day to come
When from the cold and silent tomb
A voice shall wake the dead.

—L.H. Green, Written for the Botany Club
that met in the hollow about 1897
(Hattie and Katie Ilk, Allie Anderson and Mary C. Green)

With so many of the family members in the Oakwood area, impromptu family reunion gatherings for covered dish dinners and picnics were frequent, with Herbert and Lucy bringing their girls, Emmet and Emma their children, Leslie and his family, and Father David and Augusta enjoying all their grandchildren. The pond was a favorite play area for all the children. As they got older, they built a platform in the middle to swim out to, and diving boards, high and low. The Pond had been dredged to make it deep enough to reach underground water, and after that, never did go dry. It was also used for an ice skating rink for the children on cold winter days.

Leslie Cranston had moved his law practice and family from Ohio to Gibson City. In 1904 he invited his sister Mary's family to a street fair in Gibson City. One of Vivian's first memories was watching that fair from his Uncle Leslie's law office. He watched two men on a bicycle without tires ride across a rope stretched 20 feet over the street. He also remembered a rude boy snapping the rubber band under his chin that held his hat on. Another memory of that four-year old was the beautiful leather straps that helped lower his grandfather Green's casket into the ground at his funeral.

The Green families in Oakwood often shared Sunday dinners, and the children played games in the yard. On one hide-and-seek game, Vivian remembers successfully hiding under his mother's skirt. He knew there would always be cookies in his mother's cookie jar, and once he tossed a piece to their big dog, Tramp. Alta, Esther, and their cousins played with their dolls, "Sweetheart" and the home-made "sister" dolls, dressing them for make-believe tea parties or church.

The family did visit friends and family. Lincoln drove them on the long trip to Urbana where the whole family enjoyed a rare treat of purchased hamburgers. And one early morning, before dawn, Lincoln woke and dressed Vivian. Vee remembered kissing Ruth goodbye as she slept. On a trip to Mansfield Lincoln carried him past a catalpa tree in full bloom in the moonlight. He later remembered how sweet the blossoms smelled. And Lincoln drove with Vivian on the long trip to Urbana. On *that* trip Vee was treated to popcorn. How good it smelled! He also often went with his father on the wagon loads of grain taken to the mill to be ground. Vivian laughed and clapped as his father shared stories of his childhood.

Another miniature by Mary G. Green. Date unknown.

Part IV

This Change Is Hard

Tragedy

In the early fall of 1905, Lincoln was attending a series of services at the church teaching on the "second blessing." He was eager to receive it, and lingered late in prayer, without assurance yet that he had received that baptism in the Spirit. He was confident that in the last meeting the next night, he would receive it. On the next morning, he husked corn, in the afternoon worked on the new corn crib he was building across the road east of the house. And after supper, he went as he had for the past four evenings, to the meeting at the church. He was disappointed.

It was too much for his health. The next morning while husking, he said that his father and Mary's father, both of whom had died during the last two years, suddenly appeared at his wagon, and said, "We have come to take you to heaven."

But he said to them, "I have to say goodbye to Mary," and jumped into his wagon and came home. He told Mary about his seeing the two fathers, and what they had said to him.

"The fathers didn't come right away," Mary said to him. "Lincoln, don't you think the Lord was giving you a choice, and when you came home to tell me, the Lord knew that you would prefer to live and take care of me and the children."

"They said they had come for me." Lincoln answered. "Maybe I should have gone with them?"

"Oh, Lincoln, no!" Mary briefly thought about what it would be like without Lincoln. "I love you and need you, Lincoln. The children need you. God wouldn't take you away from us now. And He is using you in the church, and so many ways here. Are you sure the two fathers were really there? It might have been just in your mind."

"They were there, Mary, and I heard what they said."

Lincoln walked to his chair in the living room and sat there until the children came home from school. After greeting them, he started walking down the road to go to church, but stopped at George Fox's home just north of the church, and lay down on their lounge.

When Lincoln left, Mary left Vivian and Richard with the older children, and followed him, calling Wilbert and Dr. Winslow from Oakwood. They met her at George Fox's home. Lincoln was asleep. After the doctor had heard the facts and examined Lincoln, he motioned for them to go into the kitchen, saying Lincoln could hear them even if he seemed to be asleep. As the four of them talked, they decided that they should take Lincoln home, and the next day, take him to the hospital for treatment of "men of unsound mind" near Chicago. Wilbert took Lincoln and Mary home in his spring wagon, and the next day drove Lincoln to the hospital in Chicago.

The day after arriving at the hospital, Lincoln seemed to be all right. He wrote Mary a normal letter, and kept writing every few days. "All but two of his letters were all right," but in those two he seemed confused. He wrote about taking walks down by the shore of Lake Michigan, thinking and praying. [All of this information is in the letter of her memories that Mary C. Green dictated to her son Roy in later years.]

In December, the hospital released him as cured, to go home for Christmas. It was a wonderful family Christmas, with the now traditional orange in the Christmas stocking toes. Alta, so full of anticipation, kept her orange until it was spoiled. The family had always been frugal, and at dinner several days after Christmas, Mary noticed Lincoln spreading his piece of bread with butter, and then adding jelly. "Two spreads on your bread?" she lovingly chastised him.

Without hesitation he answered, "I'm saving bread." Everybody laughed in appreciation. Their father was again his laughing, loving self.

The familiar routines resumed. Roy was happy to have his dad there to help with the milking and harnessing the horses for going to church. Mary felt the load of managing everything by herself eased. Lincoln seemed almost like his old self, but had long periods of silence, and seemed uncertain at times.

On Sunday morning, January 5, 1906, Mary, pregnant with their seventh child, was not feeling well. She said to Lincoln that she thought she would not go to church. He said then he would not go, either. He went out, Mary thought, to help Roy hitch Mack to the buggy for the children to go to church. She went out to tell him something—and found he was not helping Roy. Mary and Alta, hunting, found him in the west crib, where he had hanged himself in the driveway. Mary asked Alta to hold him up while she went to get a knife to cut the rope. He was still alive, but unconscious. They carried him to the house and laid him on the lounge in the living room. He did not regain consciousness and died the next morning.

In shock and dismay, Mary and Lincoln's brother Wilbert arranged the funeral service at the church. The church was full of mourning family and friends, all sad and shocked at his early death. Augusta, Lincoln's mother, sat with her son Emmet on the first row with Mary and Roy. With the rest of the children sitting behind them, Alta was holding two-year-old Richard. Augusta was still wearing black in mourning for her late husband, holding back tears with a handkerchief over her eyes.

The Reverend C.A. Dwyer preached the homily, humbly stressing Lincoln's love of the Lord and years of service in the church. "Even as a youth," he said, "Lincoln was one to be followed as a good example of the Christian life."

The obituaries in the Danville paper, repeated in the *Urbana Courier*, outlined the statistics: "Lincoln Hamlin Green, born in Xenia, Ohio, on April 4, 1863, died in his home on January 6, 1906, age 43 years, 9 months. When he was six years old, he moved with his parents from Xenia to East Bend Township, near Gibson City, where he lived with his parents until 1890. He attended Adrian College in Adrian, Michigan, intending to serve as a minister. In 1890 he married Mary Esther Cranston and the two of them attended Adrian College until, in January 1891, he became ill, and his doctor advised him to leave school and find a vocation outdoors. In September he and his wife moved to their farm near Oakwood. They moved in at Thanksgiving 1891."

After listing surviving family members, the newspaper obituary went on to describe Lincoln's life in the Oakwood area: "Lincoln Green united with the United Brethren Methodist Church at an early age, and his life has been a beautiful example of manly Christian character to all who knew him and to whomever came within his influence. As a boy and in early manhood, he was considered by his companions as one whose example could be profitably followed—'unclean' acts and thoughts were not in him.

"His home life and his association with his children were of the best, and those that knew intimately of his home life would go away from his house with better thoughts and a nobler conception of the true spirit that makes the home the bulwark of American institutions. The memories of the wise, tender associations and friendly intimacies will ever be to his wife and little ones an incentive to be like him and do better things."

"On the first of January 1906, Mr. Green began his fourteenth year as superintendent of Lake Shore Sunday School. He and his wife became members of the Lake Shore Brethren Church soon after they moved to Vermillion County. He was a constant and untiring worker in the church and Sunday School until his death. Many of his associates, old and young, will remember thankfully the impulse he gave them for better things and a truer and broader view of what man is and ought to be. Always of a religious nature, when he was forced to leave training for the ministry, he determined to do as much good as he could among his fellow men."

After the burial in the Oakwood Cemetery, Mary, who had been controlling her grief for the sake of the children, noticed Augusta sobbing uncontrollably. Losing her son so soon after her husband, was too much. In the years Lincoln had lived at home helping his father farm, she had grown especially close to him. Emmet and Emma Carpenter, with whom Augusta lived after David's death, were trying to comfort her. Mary went to her, put her arms around her mother-in-law, hugging her without saying a word. Mary's eyes were teary, but she knew she had to keep her grief in control because of her children. Her calm in their common sadness helped Augusta, and strengthened the bond between them.

After the funeral came the confusion and uncertainty. Roy was still attending the Oakwood High school, and had another two years there before graduation. Who would plant and harvest crops in Rose Haven Farm? Roy was too young, and Mary did not want him to miss his education, and he had wanted to go to college, too. Mary knew too well she alone had six children to care for, and another on the way. She could hire someone to do the farm work, or rent the land, or even sell it. No, she could not sell Rose Haven Farm, so full of love and memories.

She wanted to hide someplace and cry, but there was no time to feel sorry for herself. Where would she find the money to educate her children? Teaching would not pay enough, and she could not leave the children to work, anyway. But, she was not alone, not ever! She knew her God, and He would never leave or forsake her.

Mary Esther Cranston Green, widow, closed her eyes and prayed, "Our Father in Heaven, You have been faithful to take care of us in abundance all our lives. You know my sorrow and my concerns. Our lives are in Your hands. Show us Your plans. We are Your children and Your servants. We put our trust in You."

The family members were gathered in the house at the Rose Haven Farm after the funeral, comforting Mary and the children. Mary's younger brother Stephen, took Mary aside and said, "Mary, you'll need someone to handle the farm now. Emma and I are just renting in Gibson City. We haven't found land of our own to farm yet. We have been wondering who you would find to take over the farm, and Emma suggested we would be the best choice. Would you allow me to farm beautiful Rose Haven Farm as long as you need us?"

The tears did come into Mary's eyes then—happy tears. "Thank you, Stephen. It would help us so very much. You and Emma and little Bernice and Vera could live in the Mason house, and join us for meals if you like. And Bernice and Richard could play together, and the big girls help take care of baby Vera sometimes. Thank you. You are an answer to my prayer."

Mary had no time for tears in February and March, but she lived on prayer and the love of and for her six children. They missed their father, but they did accept the added chores. Roy was in charge of the animals, while Alta and Esther helped after school and week-ends when they could, and Mary supervised. Vivian, shortened to "Vee" had started school, and Mary found comfort in two-year-old Richard's laughter and love.

Vee was fond of playing tricks on his brother and sisters. On his way home from school one afternoon, he laid a stone he had found on the trolley track. Esther found it, took it off, and scolded him, saying that he might have caused the trolley to jump the track and tip over, injuring many passengers.

This seventh pregnancy was harder than the others. Alta tried especially hard to help and support her mother. What a relief it was when Stephen and Emma moved into the Mason house early in March. Roy was proud to show Uncle Stephen around the farm, introduce him to Mack and the other animals, all the tools, and the fields. Stephen had been farming with his father, and then on his own rented land, and he quickly planned and began the planting. Roy was proud to help Stephen after school, but his mother would not let him neglect his homework. Alta, without being asked, did most of the work in cooking and cleaning up after meals, and kept the house clean and neat. Esther fed the chickens and gathered the eggs, with Ruth helping. Emma noticed immediately that Mary was having a hard time, and worked beside her, and rested with her, watching the two toddlers, and baby Vera while sharing family memories. Stephen plowed and disced Mary's garden even before he started preparing the fields for planting. Planting the vegetable seeds in the concentric circles lifted Mary's heart. She and Emma planted enough for both families to eat all summer and can for the winter.

When school was out, the children worked and played, enjoying the pond and the three trees in the side yard. Mary supervised the chores of each, willing to delegate more tasks, because she was having trouble keeping up. Emma was a wonderful help, especially with the children and gardens.

Martin was born July 16, 1906. He was smaller than the other babies, and not as strong. Mary was grateful to have Stephen and Emma there. The household centered on Martin for a while, but the older children enjoyed the pond on the hot August days. They had built a float in the middle to swim out to. With tender care, Martin was stronger by mid September when the older children returned to school. Roy was enjoying sports in Oakwood High School, as well as his studies. Mary had transferred her love of learning to her children. All of them did well in school and loved to read.

Christmas was sad without Lincoln, bringing back too many memories, but the delight of little Richard and Bernice with his new blocks and big ball, and her new doll, and Martin shaking his new rattle, and all the new books and clothes helped. The family also took some food and clothing to some of the poor people in Oakwood. Esther was asked to play the part of Mary in the Church Christmas pageant, and Vee enjoyed pretending to be a shepherd boy.

January was also a hard month for Mary and Alta. Memories were hard to shut out. With the routine of school and chores, though, life went on, and was good. Stephen took care of spring planting, and Mary felt well again, enjoying working with Emma, Roy, and Alta getting vegetables and a few flowers planted.

Life couldn't continue, though, without complications. In March of 1907, Martin started sniffling and crying. In a few days, Mary noticed he had a little fever. It got worse, and realizing this was no common cold, Mary called Dr. Winslow. The examination was thorough. "It isn't good, Mary," he said to her. "There's been an epidemic of polio in the area, and somehow Martin has caught it."

"I've heard about polio, but I don't know much about it. How can we treat it?" Mary was concerned. She had heard of people left crippled from polio.

Dr. Winslow hesitated, reluctant to say, "Mary, there is no known treatment. All we can do is keep him as comfortable as possible, cool clothes for the fever, plenty of liquids. So far, it is a mild case. Watch him carefully. If the fever gets very high, and he seems to be in worse pain, we should get him into the hospital. This is contagious, Mary. Be careful to keep your hands clean, and keep your other children away from him." He started repacking his Medical bag, then added, "Polio often leaves disabilities. It wouldn't hurt for us to pray that Martin will recover without permanent damage."

Prayers for Martin's escape from damaging disability became a part of their morning prayers. His fever continued until nearly June, almost time for schools to close for the summer. Martin's left leg was twisted a little, and his foot numb. Dr. Winslow outlined some massage and stretching exercises in hopes of correcting the potentially crippling deformity. Mary faithfully massaged and stretched that little leg well after Martin began to walk the next summer. He had a little limp, but managed to get around well.

In June, at the start of the summer vacation, Mary called aside Stephen, Emma, and her older children, to discuss plans.

She began, "Roy, you have one more year of high school, and want to enroll in the University of Illinois after that. Before we realize it, Alta will be starting, college too, and soon all the rest. When you graduate, Roy, do you want to take over the farm, or would you like a different career?"

"Mother, I've been thinking about that. I like to build things. I had thought about engineering, but I love this farm, too. I would hate to see Rose Haven Farm belong to anyone else. Yes, I do want to come back here and farm. Besides, Mother, you love this farm, too. You made it beautiful. It will always be your home."

Mary was so proud of her son, and his answer gave her a glimpse of a happy future. She made up her mind. "I have been thinking about ways to let all of you get an education. I will go to Urbana, and buy a house. We will live there in the school terms, and come back here in the summers. We have some savings, and a house in Urbana would be an investment. Living there, we will have enough money for each and every one of you to attend college. Stephen, we appreciate your offer to help us. You didn't ask how we would make it worth-while for you. I want you to have the largest share of the sale of farm products. We will just need enough for our expenses. We are so happy to have you here helping us, and will be glad if you want to stay until Roy finishes college. You can move to the big house, and we can use the Mason House during summers to plant and grow food to can for the winters. However, if you want to leave, we will find someone to rent the farm until Roy can take over."

"Thank you, Mary." Stephen said. "We have enjoyed being with you on Rose Haven Farm, and you have done some good thinking. Some day, Emma and I will want to get our own farm, but we are happy here for now. I'll harvest the crops this fall, keep the farm in the winter, and plant in the spring, and look forward to having all of your back for the summer. Mary, Emma and I can start your summer garden for you too."

The Urbana home at Main and Cottage Grove that Mary moved her family into after Lincoln's death. This would prove to be a new beginning for the family, and provided new educational and social experiences. January 14, 1927.

At Home in Urbana

Soon after making her decision, Mary took the trolley into Urbana to look at houses. She found and bought a new house on East Main Street. Urbana, Illinois. Describing it to her family, she said, "It is a good house of four rooms and a hallway downstairs and upstairs, two large bedrooms, a small bedroom, and a very small room over the downstairs hallway. Each of the three larger bedrooms has a large closet.

In mid-September, Stephen and Wilbert helped load the Green family furniture into two spring wagons, and Mary and her seven children moved to their new home. As they walked up the five steps to the front porch, Ruth discovered the swing on the left side. Richard joined her, gently swinging back and forth. Roy had noticed the carriage house in back, and took off to explore it. Mary laughed at the excitement of her little ones, as she entered the house with Alta, Esther and Vivian. Alta immediately noted the stained glass in the front door, and stairs from the front hall, and the large living room with a fireplace. Esther had walked on into the dining area, and called for Alta to come and see the built-in cupboards under the three windows. As they walked back to the kitchen, Alta went to the sink, and turned on the faucet. "We have water here! We don't have to bring it from a well! Just like in the church."

There were two doors in the kitchen. Esther opened one. "It's a pantry. Lots of room for storage."

"The other door leads to the back yard. Come, see, there's a downstairs bedroom, too, just like at the farm." Mary said as she led them back through the dining room to the room on the other side of the entry hall, and then up the stairs.

Vivian had been exploring, too. He had found the door to the basement stairs, ventured down them, and returned to exclaim, "There's a furnace downstairs! And a little room with a little metal door instead of a window. There are two big sinks, too, and a back door." He joined the rest of the family to explore the upstairs. But just then, Stephen and Wilbert brought Martin in. He had been sleeping in the makeshift bed in the wagon. They were eager to begin unloading the furniture so they could return before dark.

Mary handed Martin to Alta, saying, "Take care of him, Alta, as you look at the upstairs. I'll stay here to tell the men where the furniture goes." She looked around for Roy. "Vivian, find Roy, and you two help your uncles bring in the furniture."

With four of them working, it didn't take long to get the needed furniture into the correct rooms. There were boxes to unpack, but that could wait. Mary found the picnic lunch she had packed, and they all sat around the dining table eating the sandwiches and fruit. Alta hunted for the box with the glasses, and brought water from the kitchen faucet for each to drink. Roy had found a bucket in the pile of tools, and took water out for the horses.

Mary hugged to her brother and brother-in-law, thanking them for their help, also thanking God for loving families. Now she was on her own, but in a nice home. The children went to the front porch to say goodbye and watch the wagons pull away.

Back in the dining room, Mary gathered her children together, and gave them directions. Until we get everything unpacked and put away, all of you stay in the house. Ruth, you watch Richard as you unpack. Roy, you take the boxes to the right rooms—I have them marked—and then help me unpack household goods. Alta, you unpack the dishes and kitchen ware, and arrange them in the cupboards. Esther, will you take care of the bedding and the clothes in the girls' room. I'll put mine away later. My room is the small one. The girls have the largest room with the two beds. Vivian, you take care of putting the clothes away in the boys' room, and put the towels in the bathroom closet. Ruth, you and Richard take care of unpacking the toys. I think one of these cupboards in the dining room would be a good place for some of the toys.

Roy, we'll take care of lamps and other household goods. Wait! I don't want you wandering off and getting lost. Until you know exactly where everything is around here, I want all of you to stay in the house or yard."

With everyone helping, it didn't take too long to get everything unpacked and in place. Mary went around checking the drawers, closets and cupboards. Alta had the food easy to find, and while Mary took care of Martin, she and Esther prepared supper. As they gathered around the table, Mary gave the blessing, "Dear Lord, Thank you for providing for us this home and getting our belongings here and in place. Bless our new home and all of us in it. We are yours, and in your hands. Show us how to serve You in this new place, guide and protect us here, and help us to find your choice of new friends. Bless this food for our use."

After supper, they all went out to the porch in the cool September evening. Mary sat on the swing holding Martin, with Richard and Ruth, while the others sat on the steps. Mr. and Mrs. Villiars came to welcome them. Mr. Villiars, grey headed with a reddish face and a big smile, said he had lived in Urbana all his life, but had just bought his home here a year ago. He owned a small hardware store. Mrs. Villiars, a warm and friendly heavy-set woman said she helped in the store now that their children were all grown and away. She had baked chocolate cookies for them, which all the Green children enjoyed. Mrs. Villiars offered to show them around the town the next day.

After watching the sunset, Mary took Martin and Richard upstairs to the little bedroom. The very little bedroom held the crib for Richard. He protested that he was not a baby anymore. The room was not big enough for a real bed, Mary explained. "We'll leave the side down, You can get in and out by yourself. Soon I'll see if we can get a real bed small enough to fit in your room. You are a big boy now." She gave him a hug, and he willingly climbed into his open crib.

Mary changed Martin into his nightwear, and put him to bed in her single bed. Then she arranged her clothes in the small chest and closet, and climbed into bed beside him, careful not to waken him. She was tired!

The three girls in the east room, which was large enough for two beds and a dresser, decided that the two older ones would sleep in the double bed and Ruth in the single. They talked together about their hopes for their new school and new friends before falling asleep. The two older boys, Roy and Vivian shared a bed in the other large room. The next morning Mary and the children gathered around the table for devotions as usual. Each day, one of them would read the designated chapter, discuss any new or valued information, and then eat their breakfast. Then it was time for the family to explore the neighborhood. The house was on a corner lot, and diagonally across the street, the little Grace Methodist Church. The neighborhood was full of houses similar to theirs, two-story frame houses, most with porches and small yards. It wasn't very far from a downtown area with small stores, and in the other direction, a meeting of several streets and the highway out of town. A trolley line was just a block away. It would be a convenient location, but they didn't find any schools.

After lunch, as she had promised, Mrs. Villiars came over to get them oriented with the town. She stayed long enough to tell them where all the schools were, and describe the new preparatory school at the University. Roy was quite interested. Would it be possible for him to go there for his last year of high school? It was! And there was a good new school, Thornburn High School, for the girls. Vivian—who now *insisted* on being called Vee, and Ruth could attend a grade school only five blocks away.

On Sunday, the Green family walked across the street to enroll in Sunday School in the Grace Methodist Church. The warm welcome gave hope of good friends. Richard was a little reluctant to stay without his mother in the toddler's class, but when he saw a toy train, he was quick to play with it. The cradle class welcomed year-old Martin and his mother enthusiastically. It was always hard to find people willing to care for the little ones. They all stayed for church, familiar in the order of worship.

Mary and Roy took the trolley to the University on Monday morning. Roy was able to enroll in the University of Illinois Preparatory School. Mary took him to the book store on the corner of Green Street to get his text books. It was a long walk, but Roy was used to that. He disdained the trolley as he started school on Tuesday.

Alta and Esther were delighted with the new high school on Race Street in Urbana, and Ruth and Vivian appreciated the shorter walk to the grade school.

City life was different from the farm. There were still chores, but much easier. There were no chickens, and that meant no eggs, no roasters. There was no garden, only the store of canned goods. They did not need a horse and buggy, for the schools were within walking distance, and the church diagonally across the street. The trolley was handy if they wanted to ride for a nickel to the University or Champaign. Mary looked over the small yard. There was a little space between the house and the carriage- house, for a small garden in the spring. Roy would have to cut the grass in the yard. They would have to buy a small grass mower. They all enjoyed the big front porch in the September evenings. The coal furnace in the basement interested Roy. It didn't' take him long to discover how to use it, but they would have to order coal. He had figured that that little room with the metal door was a coal bin. He would shovel the coal as the man of the house, but he would show his mother and Alta how to shovel coal, too. The bathroom was especially welcome. With running water, hot and cold, and a tub! Mary really appreciated the running water in the kitchen, and the laundry tubs in the basement.

Even with the two little boys at home, Mary had more time to sew with the treadle sewing machine Lincoln had bought for her. The extra room downstairs became her sewing room. She had made clothes for her children, usually sewing at night after they were in bed, but now she had time to sew in daylight! She also learned to braid rugs, not with the usual three strands, but with seven stands! She did get involved right away with the cradle class at church, and occasionally attended the Ladies' Aid in evenings when Alta could care for the little ones.

She missed her garden, but she had brought with her the lemon tree she had started from that first lemon for lemonade at her second picnic with Lincoln, and the orange tree from their first Christmas oranges. They were in the bay window in the living room.

They lived frugally—"Waste not, want not." The prosperous years had provided savings enough to buy the house, groceries and pay for the utilities, coal, and school expenses, and with the sale of the fall crops, Stephen sent the agreed-upon share of profits. She did not have to worry. Mary was a good manager, and each school child had a small allowance. They had to buy their meat and milk from a grocery store in the shopping area. On Saturdays, Alta would often go to the store to buy a five-pound roast for Sunday dinner costing $.50. There would be leftovers for sandwiches.

The children adapted to "city life" quickly. They made new friends, and found their country schools had given them an education just as good as those in the city schools. Alta especially enjoyed the larger library at school, and found that Urbana had a town library, too. Roy was able to take more science classes at the Preparatory school than had been offered in the Oakwood High School. The church, so close, also provided enjoyable activities and friends.

Emma invited them to the farm for Thanksgiving. They took the trolley! The children found it a great adventure, watching fields and houses spin past them. It was not too long a walk down the road to the farm. They enjoyed being back on the Rose Haven Farm, climbing trees, watching turtles and fish in the pond, and visiting the familiar animals. It was not as warm, though, except in the kitchen and around the stoves. They played with Bernice and Vera, and ate the generous servings of turkey, dressing, and pumpkin pie. Mary carried back generous supplies of potatoes, corn and beans, eggs, and a chicken Emma had killed and dressed for her. They were all happy to take the trolley back to their warm house.

Mary made great plans for Christmas. She was lonely for her family. She invited Wilbert and Lucy with their girls, and her mother, Artemissa, and Clara Jeanette who had come back from Kansas and Utah after the death of her husband. With her two boys, Earl and Kim, she was living with her mother, taking care of her. Clara's daughter, had died just a year after her birth.

Mary found herself singing again as she made or bought gifts for each one in the family, and as she and her children planned for the large family gathering. They would have a large tree, and bring out the treasured ornaments, and make more. She planned the meals carefully, making sure there would be plenty. Christmas cookies, made in advance, and some fudge were packed in tins saved from year to year. The children loved to help with these, taking turns licking the bowls.

Learning, Labor, and Love

In December of 1907, Roy learned that he had done so well in the University Preparatory School that he could begin college in January of 1908. As he discussed his plans and his dreams with the freshman advisor, he decided to seek his degree in agriculture, but add some courses in engineering as his electives. He was a tall, handsome young man, with a hint of a curl in his dark hair, blue, penetrating eyes, and a ready smile. He had wanted to take eighteen hours of credit, but his advisor strongly urged him to limit his courses to 15 in his first semester. The trolley went from near his home to the campus, but most of the time he chose to walk the two miles.

Roy looked for part-time work to earn a little spending money, and was offered a Saturday job working on the Morrow Plots, an area of experimental farming established at the very beginning of the college. It did not pay very much, but Roy decided that learning about new discoveries in farming would be an advantage when he took over the Rose Haven Farm. The lamp on his table in the sewing room often burned late as he faithfully prepared his homework. It wasn't very long until he was asking some pretty co-eds out for dates once in a while.

Enjoying the greater variety in the classes at the new Thornburn High School, Alta and Esther quickly adjusted, and found their education in the Oakwood schools made their classes easy. Alta was a bit shy at first, but found friends at school. She was slender, with curls in her long blond hair framing delicate features and blue eyes. She loved to read, and soon discovered the Urbana Public Library to augment the selections in her school library. She did not enter into many of the extra-curricular activities because she knew she was needed to help her mother with the two little boys and taking care of the house. Esther, on the other hand, with her darker hair and bolder features, was outgoing and joined the student chorus and debating club. Alta was the scholar, earning straight A's.

Ruth, already a beauty at eleven, walked to her grade school with Vee. Ruth was friendly and very considerate of others, even at her early age. Although she did not take her courses too seriously, she was intelligent and did well in her classes. Vee soon led in sports at recess and won over his teachers with his winning personality.

Mary was enjoying an easier life. The two little ones at home played together in peace most of the time. Richard was more serious, apt to ask penetrating questions for a toddler, and he was protective of Martin, who was now walking with a bit of a limp, but didn't seem to realize anything wrong. Mary was faithful to stretch and massage his left leg and foot every day. With an eye on the children, Mary challenged herself to weave strips of heavy old, worn-out clothes into rugs.

The lemon tree now sat in the bay window in the living room. Window sills were filled with plants. Mary sometimes bought flower pots, but more often used cups without handles and jars with cracked tops as planters. Everything seemed to flourish. With Alta taking care of Richard and Martin, Mary joined The Ladies Aid of the little Methodist Church diagonally across the street.

Faith was the foundation of this Green family. As Lincoln had started the custom, the family got up early and held devotions every morning. Mary asked the five older children in turn to read the chosen Scripture. Then they discussed it, shared their prayer needs, and prayed together every morning. Sundays, dressed in their best, the family walked over for Sunday school and church. Mary was in charge of the Primary and Infant Department, and usually teaching one of the classes when the regular teacher was absent. She often invited the preacher for Sunday dinner afterwards, too. Wanting her children to have some input from the masculine side, Mary also often invited a teacher for dinner on Sundays. One Sunday, Alta was quietly amused at the Mathematics teacher from her high school remarking that he didn't read the papers or any books outside his specialty because brains were limited in the amount of information they could absorb, and he wanted to keep his free for mathematics. After he left, Mary made it clear to her children that their brains were large enough to hold all the information they could accumulate.

Mary Esther Cranston Green tried to keep in close touch with her family, now scattered widely, but still with quite a few within traveling distance. For Thanksgiving, she would give or accept invitations from her sister Lucy and Wilbert Green and their daughters—now four, or from her brother Stephen and Emma at Rose Haven Farm, or her mother, Artemissa and her sister, Clara Jeanette and her two sons from Gibson City. Sometimes Lincoln's mother, Augusta Green, would visit. The children loved both grandmothers. Christmas was always special, with as many family members together as could crowd in the host house. But the best times were the family reunions at the farm every other summer. The cousins made close friends with those in their age groups. In these college years for her older children, Mary was trying to set traditions to keep the large families together.

Roy was determined to learn everything he could about farming. He tolerated the required reading and writing in his English and history classes, but relished the mathematics and science. He shared new information in Botany and geology with his mother, and was especially excited about the Morrow Plot experiments to improve crops. His Saturday work at the Morrow plots gave him valuable experience in crop science. In his sophomore year, he was a little impatient at adjusting schedules because he was off the usual pattern of classes, and planned with his mother to stay in Urbana for summer classes. He persuaded her, saying then he could graduate in the spring of 1911, and work together with Stephen on weekends to plant the crops, taking over the farm in June 1911 instead of in January of 1912.

In the fall of 1909, on Saturday nights Roy started attending the Epworth League College Mixer Group at the new Methodist Church on Race Street near downtown Urbana. He would often ask one of the co-eds to have an ice cream with him after the meeting, but not too often the same one. In mid December, a new young lady caught everybody's attention. Her bouffant red hair was a dramatic contrast with her classic features. Her waistline was tiny, and she walked with the grace of a professional dancer. He overheard her say to another co-ed that she had just come from Indiana, De Paul University, and intended to register at the University of Illinois in January. He tried to break into the group of college students that surrounded her, but she said goodbye to them and left before he could politely reach her alone. The next Saturday night, Roy was at the college meeting early, watching the door for her arrival. She glided in, smiling and ready to meet new friends. Roy greeted her with, "Welcome to Urbana. I heard that you come from De Paul. I hope you're going to stay for a while. I'm Roy Green."

She laughed, saying, "I'm Della Reichard. Yes, I do intend to register in January and finish my education, I'm glad to meet you, Roy."

Roy didn't waste much time asking her if he could take her home after the meeting, stopping for some ice cream. "Not tonight, Roy, I have to stay to practice my song for tomorrow morning, but another night I'd be glad to accept your invitation." He was still talking with Della, getting acquainted when the meeting started. She turned with a smile to sit next to her friends Alice and Janet.

The next morning Roy excused himself from walking across the street to the little church, and walked to the bigger new one. He sat inconspicuously near the back waiting to hear Della sing. He was not disappointed. Della had the assurance of one accustomed to performing, standing straight with a calm smile while the organist played the introduction. Her soprano voice was warm and full, words clear, tone true. He knew good voices from listening to his father's tenor voice. She was a professional! Roy was just a country boy seeking an education. Della wouldn't be interested in him! When the service was over, Roy left, hiding in the crowd.

It was hard for Roy to concentrate in class, and as he paged through his homework, he found himself trying to sketch a picture of Della. It wasn't very good. He had to pay attention on Saturday to the working of the soil in the Morrow Plots for records of the exact proportions of fertilizer and mulch were part of the experimentations. But that night, he dressed in his best and walked to the new Methodist Church, thinking of ways to remind Della that he wanted to take her for an ice cream after the service. He had never been concerned about his words with any other girl, but Della was different. She was a lady with a capital "L." Should he mention he'd heard her sing?

But Della wasn't there! Roy asked Alice about her, and learned that she had gone back to Indiana for Christmas with her parents at their family farm. She had been visiting her grandparents in Urbana, and decided then to enroll in the University. Roy knew his mother had grown up on a farm, and attended three colleges. And she had been willing to live on a farm. Maybe Della, with all her grace, would not disdain dating a farmer. He asked Alice out for ice cream, and walked her home, but learned nothing more about Della.

Christmas was a busy time with Mary's mother, Artemissa Atwood and her sister Clara Jeanette with her two boys sharing the holidays. Vee slept with Roy, and Ruth's bed was crowded into the boy's room for their cousins. Alta and Esther made room for Ruth in their bed. Mary purchased another double bed for the sewing room, realizing that many times she would need extra beds. It was a special time for Mary to share with her mother the adjustment to losing her mate. She had not felt free to talk about it, with so much responsibility, so many children to comfort and rear. Clara Jeanette, too, could share her loss, way out in Utah with two children to raise. She said she could have found a teaching position, and cared for her children, but with her father's death, it seemed right for her to return to Gibson City to be with her mother. That's family! Mary thought. How blessed they were to be part of loving families. Somehow, there was a little weight lifted from her shoulders.

After her mother and Clara Jeanette left, Mary remembered a poem she had written in Antioch College, and found it expressed the feelings she had kept concealed during the last few years:

Gethsemane

Gloomy Gethsemane, dark are the shadows
When human friendship and love wholly fail,
When they grow weary and watch not one hour
Or proffer false lips in bitter betrayal.
Bitter Gethsemane, garden of sorrow,
Many the hearts that have struggled therein,
Broken and bruised by somebody's madness,
Crushed by the weight of somebody's sin.
Awful Gethsemane,
There the dear Lord in agony prayed
With heartbreak and soul break
That the full cup from His lips might be stayed.
Sacred Gethsemane.
Take if thou wilt Thy friend to the gateway,
but enter alone To the infinite God with thy infinite pain
And pray in submission His will to be done.

Now that pain was shared, and lightened. Mary thought about how well faith and poetry both played such a helpful part in her life. She had heard the announcements from the pulpit of a new Bible Study being offered by a church member who also wrote poetry. Maybe, if Alta were willing to watch the little ones and put them to bed, she could attend it. She could use a little stimulation for her faith. God had been faithful, but was she giving enough time to Him? Alta was willing, and Mary decided she would join that group in January.

Just before Christmas, the boys especially, were delighted when it snowed. Mary and Clara Jeanette joined all the children making snowmen, remembering the Christmas when the Atwood family and Lincoln and Wilbert made the snow family in their front yard in Gibson City. Artemissa watched from the swing until she felt chilled, and retreated to the rocking chair near the fireplace in the living room. On Christmas Eve, after attending the pageant at the church, and praising Esther and Vivian for their parts, they all sang carols around the Christmas tree with the enticing packages stacked around the trunk. Clara Jeanette and Mary stayed up late, insisting Roy go to bed, too, to see that the boys didn't get too rough. The women talked and talked about their childhood, their husbands, finding solace in their children after the death of their husbands, and their plans for the future. Mary had so missed having anyone to talk to, heart to heart. They put the oranges and candy in the stockings, and hugged long and hard before they went to bed.

Christmas morning with little children is always special. They gathered for the traditional reading of the Christmas story from Luke, and then let them enjoy the treats in the stockings before they gathered for their special breakfast of caramel rolls with pecans. Afterwards, they began opening the presents. Happiness is bringing happiness to others, Mary thought. Martin was old enough to squeal in delight as he tore open the package and found the teddy bear. He stacked the blocks over and over, and knocked them down with a laugh. Richard delighted in the wagon, all his own. He had played with Roy's metal one, but this was his! He loaded it with marbles, and dumped them all over the floor, laughing, crawling after them and gathering them to do it all again. The older boys had their games, and shared in playing them, one after another. Mary had made new dresses for the girls, an annual tradition, shirts for the boys, and knitted hats and mufflers for everyone. There were also molasses cookies, but it had to be from store-bought molasses. Her children had all made or found gifts for Mary, too. Any gift made with love is dearer than one bought as a responsibility, Mary thought as she slipped the necklace Alta had made for her from gathered seeds. Christmas is the time to appreciate the love of God in sending His Son for his beloved man, and to show and share the love of family.

Mary said goodbye to her guests and put the house back to order with a lighter heart. She was going to learn again, this time in a special Bible Study. The first meeting exceeded her hopes! She felt so much closer to God, and ready to release to Him all the pent-up questions and disappointments of her life, and begin again. On January 14, as she was ironing, she thought through all the changing ideas, thoughts, emotions of her life, gathering in the form of a poem, consecrating all her life to the Lord. She put down the iron and wrote down the thoughts in a poem.

Consecration

I bring my alabaster box
Dear Lord, and break it at Thy feet.
O, may it be as good to
Thee As costly incense sweet.
For in it I have kept with care
The precious things that all the years
Of life have brought to me—
The mingled hopes and fears.
My childish fancies of Thyself,
Youth's longing to attain,
The wiser dreams of womanhood,

Ambitions that remain,
The happiness from field and sky,
The gladness of the spring,
The uplift from all outdoor things
The passing seasons bring.
The bitterness of a love that was,
Dried rose leaves of the past,
The grief that brought Thee near to me,
The shadows round me cast,
The sacred thoughts of motherhood,
The cares, the strength it brought,
The finite blent with infinite,
The wisdom dearly bought,
The present duties to be done,
Occasions to be seized,
The busy days for hands and brain,
The hunger unappeased,
The burden of the coming years,
The hope of joys to be—
These are the measure of my life—
I bring them all to Thee.

Somehow, the burden she had been carrying was now lifted. All this now was in the hands of the Lord, and He loved her, and would guide and strengthen her. He had taken over the load of responsibilities she was trying to carry all by herself. Mr. Hemlock did make assignments for meditations on Mark: 4, the 23rd Psalm, and suggest other topics, like Communion, and Mary found both enjoyment and appreciation from her teacher for the many poems she wrote.

After Christmas, Roy had to concentrate on studying for his mid-term examinations. He was not worried, for he was a good student and faithfully did his homework He was planning on continuing to take a fuller schedule, determined to finish a semester early. He was also wondering how soon Della would come back from Indiana, and whether she would be living in Urbana, and continue coming to the Epworth League meetings.

He had to wait until the third Saturday in January for the College Class meeting. He made himself wait until the group had already gathered, then greeted his friends, and looked eagerly around the room. Della was there, talking with Alice. He walked over to talk to the two of them. They both looked up with smiles. "It's good to see you again. It's been a long time since our last meeting. I hope you both had wonderful Christmases. Della, I heard you went back to Indiana. Did you decide to enroll in Illinois this semester."

"Hello, Roy," Della said. "Yes, I'm going to take a little art."

"My mother studied oil painting and pottery here the first year the University admitted women." Roy added, "I'm sure you'll like it." He noticed Alice looking down, and asked, "Alice, what are you taking this semester?"

"I've decided to make history my major. It's American and Ancient, the new and the old this semester." Alice added, "Della, why study art? What can you do with that?"

Roy noticed Della was a little upset by the question, and quickly said, "Art is important. It adds beauty to our lives, and then work isn't so much of a burden. That's what my mother has taught us."

Della gave a special smile to Roy, and commented, "Nature is so beautiful. I want to be able to capture it in pictures to keep the wonder in my memory. Alice, if I learn how to appreciate great art, and how to paint, I could teach others." Then she turned to Roy, saying, "Your mother must be a wonderful woman."

"I think so. I'd like for you to meet her." Just then, they were called to take their seats. The meeting was beginning. Roy was glad. He wanted to ask Della if he could take her home, but didn't want to do it with Alice there.

After the meeting, Roy found Della alone, putting on her coat. Roy held it for her, and took his coat off the hook, saying, "Della, would you let me take you home tonight, and maybe stop for some ice cream?"

"I'd like that, Roy, but maybe hot cocoa instead of ice cream." She laughed with Roy at the reminder of the cold. It was cold and they did enjoy the hot drinks. Della was staying with her grandparents at 210 South Grove Street, not too far southeast of the church. It was a three-story house with a porch across the front, and left side. Della shared with Roy the challenge her father had faced. He had been "a math whiz" in his one-room grade school, so talented in mathematics that when he finished the eighth grade, he was asked to take a position teaching mathematics in that same school.

Amazed at the similarity, Roy shared the fact that his mother, too, had been asked to teach in her one-room school the year after she finished eighth grade. "Did your father go on to study and make teaching his career?" Roy asked.

Della hesitated, and shook her head sadly. "No. He taught a few years, and got tired of it. He went home to help his father with his farm and never did go on to school. When his father died, he just took over the farm. He married, and we grew up on that farm. But that did cause him to want me to get an education. He sent me to DePaul University, but it was too expensive for him to continue tuition, room, and board.

Grandma Reichard invited me to stay with her, so here I am."

Roy felt free to share his story. "I grew up on a farm, too," and Roy proceeded to tell the story of how his parents started Rose Haven Farm. "I intend to farm there when I finish college." After a bit of silence, he added, "The farm is called The Rose Haven Farm. My mother is really good with plants, and she took a truck-load of dead-looking rose sticks, rooted them and planted roses all along the road and driveway. They are dying out now, but it was beautiful."

"It must have been lovely. I like that name for a farm. You must have a good Father, too, to send you to college. Not all farmers value lots of schooling."

Roy was impressed with Della's appreciation of education. "Your father does, Della. Mine did too, but he died in 1906."

"You live in town. Did your mother have to sell the farm—no, you said you were going to farm it after you finish college." Della was wondering.

"My uncle is farming it until I finish school. Mother bought a house here in Urbana so all seven of us could go to college. She knew she could not afford room and board for each of us in turn." Roy was surprised at how much he was sharing with Della, but she made it so easy.

"Seven? And all to college? What a challenge for your mother!" Roy had never really thought about how hard it would be for his mother. She always seemed to be calm and assured. One thing he did know, he wanted to see Della again. Before he left, he asked her if he could take her home next Saturday night, too.

That spring semester, Roy and Della had many Saturday nights together, and Roy also took her to one of the Star Course concerts on campus—started in 1892—featuring a well-known opera star.

What a special evening that was! Della enjoyed it so much that Roy made an effort to find another musical program. There was a concert by the University Chorus, and after enjoying the program, Roy suggested that she might enjoy trying out for the chorus the next semester. Her voice would be an asset to any group.

"If I can come back next semester I'll certainly try that."

"Della, I didn't like that *if*. You have to come back. Indiana's too far away." Roy had already assumed he would have two more years to be with Della, and just maybe, more.

"Roy, college costs money, even when I stay with my grandparents. Farmers don't have a lot of extra money." Della was considerate of her parents, Roy had to admit.

"Couldn't you find a job, Della, to help with expenses? You wanted to learn enough about art to be able to teach it. Please find some way to be here next year, too." Roy was a little amazed about how much he wanted her to come back.

Later, remembering she was singing in the church choir, he made an effort to go to the new church just to hear her, and with his mother's permission, he asked Della to come to their house for Sunday dinner in May.

Mary was happy to have the chance to meet the woman who had so impressed Roy. He had not talked very much about her, but he had commented on how much Della and her family had in common with Mary and his father.

As Roy and Della arrived after church that Sunday, Roy was proud to introduce her to his mother and all his brothers and sisters. Alta was especially interested in her college classes. "Are you taking oil painting, Della? Mother studied that at the University in 1890!"

"Yes, Alta, that's one of my courses. I really enjoy it. I'm also studying art history and design." Della was enthusiastic. "Roy told me about your mother." Della turned to Mary, "Mrs. Green, are you still painting?"

"No, Della. There just isn't time raising seven children. It did help me to enjoy art, though, and appreciate talent in others. I guess my gardening and sewing benefit from my love of art. Are you considering being an artist as a career?"

Della laughed. "Artists are usually struggling to survive. I'll probably try teaching. I heard you were a teacher."

"Yes, I taught one-room schools for six years. I liked it all right, but I was planning to get more education so I could teach in higher education. Then Lincoln asked me to marry him, and that was definitely the better choice." Mary thought back to her wondering why Lincoln waited so long to ask, and facing a life without him. How she missed him! She shook her head a little, and asked, "Your father was a teacher too, wasn't he?"

"He was so young, just twelve when he started teaching, and seventeen when he quit. I sometimes think he regretted that he started teaching so young and missed high school. I don't think he's very fond of farming. He loves to read."

"Sometimes we don't get our first choice, but God can bless us in whatever career we're following," Mary said, "I'm sure he's very proud of you as you pursue your educational goals. Tell me about your mother."

Della smiled. "Flavia, that's her name. She and my father met in church soon after Ves, my father, came back to help Grandfather John farm. She finished high school, but didn't go on to school. They were so much in love and married just a year after they met. They're still quite devoted to each other. She seems to enjoy gardening, taking care of the chickens, and the home. She's a very good cook, and a good Mother for me and my sisters and brothers."

Mary wondered how she would have felt if she had never gone on to college. She didn't graduate, but her college years had meant a lot to her.

Roy commented, "Della's grandparents are very special people, Mother. They moved here from Indiana soon after Mr. Reichard came back to the farm. He bought a grain elevator, and started buying and selling stocks on margin. He made money most of the time, but lost some, too. Her grandmother is president of the Ladies' Aid in the Methodist Church. She plays the piano, too. She grew up in Champaign with her parents."

Della was interested, too, in learning about the Rose Haven Farm. After dinner Della enjoyed talking to the children, especially sharing favorite books with Alta. Mary was very happy to meet Della, noticing, too, how very fond of her Roy was.

When the semester was over, Roy reluctantly said goodbye to Della. She was going home for the summer, hoping to come back in the fall. Roy was eager to get back to the farm. He did love that place, and in the quiet times, he and his brothers and sisters would enjoy that pond and the animals. There was a satisfaction in seeing that black dirt turn under the plow, catching weeds, but leaving the corn stalks, and in pitching the hay into the hay loft. It would even be good seeing the milk squirt into the pail as he milked the cows.

But he had only a short time there. He was determined to go to summer school. Even with eighteen hours a semester, he would need a few more to graduate in June of 1911. He arranged with his mother to stay in the Urbana house, and the University was happy to have him working part time in the Morrow Plots for a little extra money to buy food and eat out occasionally. It was a good summer for him to live independently, and even learn to cook a little and keep up a house and yard.

On the farm, his mother's garden flourished. Home-grown tomatoes and beans were somehow better than store-bought or canned, and fresh eggs and fried chicken a treat.

In September, after a few weeks back at the farm, Roy and the family were glad to return to the Urbana home. Roy enjoyed learning. He signed up again for eighteen hours credit, now assured that he would graduate in June of 1911.

It was time for Richard to start to school. He was excited to join the "big" members of his family. Martin missed him, though, and when he came home after school, he spent time teaching Martin what he was learning. One day just after school, Mary saw the two little boys concentrating on the Bible. She watched quietly for a while, seeing them quickly turn pages, writing something on a piece of paper. Her curiosity won. She asked, "Richard, you can't read the Bible that fast, can you?"

"Of course not, Mama. I'm teaching Martin to add the numbers of pages in the books. Jude only has one!"

"You're learning addition really fast, Richard. And you'll teach Martin to learn fast, too. I'm proud of you." Mary glanced at the figures. They weren't very accurate.

When the college church group started, Roy was disappointed to find that Della was not there. Alice informed him that Della could not enroll this semester. He didn't even have an address in Indiana to write her. He invited Alice to share an ice cream with him, and asked her to get an address for him from Della's grandparents. A week later Alice gave him the address and Roy began correspondence for the semester. He learned she was teaching art to a group of high school girls, planning to return to college when she had enough money for tuition. It was a long semester. But in January Roy did find Della back in Urbana with her grandmother, and she enrolled in the University.

That made it a satisfying year. He was helping to plan the Morrow Plots, learning how to choose the crops for rotation for optimal use of the soil, what fertilizers were preferable—the practical to join with the book knowledge. He learned, too, in his engineering classes, about building, power sources, electricity and water control. But best of all, Della was there, and he was in love. Saturday night dates, and Sunday dinners at his home or at her grandparent's with Della brightened the year.

As he had planned, Roy went back to the farm on his Easter vacation to help with the spring plantings. Mary chose to stay in town with the other children, busy in the church. She had found her peace and was planting a small garden behind the house, and thinking of the sadness of planting that first garden there right after Lincoln's death. That evening she wrote down her feelings:

My Easter

I knelt one day in my garden path
Beside a desolate bed,
Where plants once bent with fragrant bloom
Stood straight and bare, some dead.
The birds were flitting from shrub to shrub,
The sun lay warm on the ground.
And I was not sad with thoughts of the past
Tho' none of its beauty I found;

For under the leaves I knew that the bulbs
Were lifting their blossoms fair,
And the rich dark earth had softened been
For new hopes to be planted there.
Today I knelt in that path again
To gather my daffodils
With their silver stars and golden cups;
Their fragrance the garden fills.
And I know that after the winters of life
God gives us beautiful springs
If we yield our bared hearts to the warmth of
His love And nurture the seed that He brings.

Roy invited Della to his senior prom, bought her a corsage, and met her with his dreams. But when he asked her to marry him, Della said she was not yet ready to settle down. She had been offered a teaching position in her Indiana high school and wanted to take it. Disappointed, Roy had to settle for farming by himself, with only letters from Della.

Mary had the satisfaction of two graduations in June. Roy received his degree in Agriculture from the University of Illinois, and Alta was Valedictorian of her class at Thornburn High School. Roy, after helping Uncle Stephen with the planting on the farm, was eager to take over the responsibility. Uncle Stephen had bought a farm in Arkansas, also eager to establish his family there. He and Emma moved there in June to tend crops he had planted after those in Rose Haven Farm were planted with Roy in Easter vacation.

Roy had a very busy summer. Vee was a little help with the farming, but still too young for heavy work. The girls helped Mary with the garden, chickens and, of course, cooking and housework. They did a lot of the things he would have to handle after September. Roy wondered what it would be like in the winter doing it all by himself. He might find a hired man part time. He would probably need only one cow. Mary and Roy worked together to set up the records and accounts. Stephen had left good books, and Roy learned quickly. His mother was still the owner, but Roy intended to buy the farm when he got settled, and make it his own. The neighbors had always gathered at the farms in turn for the wheat harvesting. The women prepared generous noon dinners, a time for fellowship and a little rest before returning to the hot fields. Although Mary and the girls were old hands at preparing for the harvesting crew, it was a new challenge for Roy to be the host in charge of the harvesting of his crop instead of just a helper.

Adding Illini

Back in Urbana, it was time for Alta to register at the University. After she finished registering, she looked over a bulletin board nearby, and saw a little notice: "Position open for assistant clerk for Miss Mathews, Dean of Women." She could do that! Without even asking her mother, she found the Dean's office, and applied for the position. Alta was a quiet, gentle girl, mature and competent from the responsibilities she had had as the oldest girl in a large family. Her record of honors in her high school class also recommended her. She was hired for part time work, keeping records and grading papers. As she started her classes, she also started a record book of her income and expenses. She even noted saving her nickel for carfare and buying an occasional ice cream cone to augment her bag lunch.

Alta managed to keep a straight A record, please the Dean of Women, and be asked to return to the job in September. The summer on the farm was busy, but filled with joy of family and the Sunday afternoon picnics and walks in the woods, looking for birds and wild flowers. It was almost like the summers before her father died. She determined to study botany next year. She also learned to use her mother's treadle sewing machine, making two new dresses for the next year. In September, Alta was eager to return to college. She loved to learn, and even enjoyed her work with the Dean of Women. She still hurried home to help her mother.

The Christmas of 1912 Mary decided to spend at the farm to be with Roy and the relatives living in the Oakwood area. Mary thought from his letters that Roy was lonely. They all enjoyed being back on the farm. The pond was frozen, ready for ice skating, and they all spent time making gifts for everyone or wrapping the ones they had been working on all fall. Mary enjoyed baking the cookies and planning a Christmas dinner. And it was a wonderful Christmas with all the family traditions, the tree with its candles, stockings with an orange in the toe and candy and little toys, church and carols. But the most exciting gift came three days after Christmas. Roy received a letter, and after reading it he was speechless. Finally he managed to say, "She said yes. I'm to meet her in Urbana to make plans."

He handed his mother the letter, and she confirmed the news. Roy had been begging Della to marry him in every letter, and finally she was ready. She had enjoyed teaching, but missed him, and she was already in Urbana with her grandmother and grandfather. She asked him to come there to make plans for the wedding. Roy, usually not very emotional, was grinning and barely restrained himself from jumping up and down. He was ready to pack a bag and get on the trolley that day. Mary persuaded him to write a note that he would be there right after New Years' Day, and do a little preparation to receive her in his home after their marriage. Mary, too wanted a few days to make sure the kitchen and house were in order for a bride, and the master bed room beautiful with special curtains, the best bedspread, and plenty of room in the closet. Just before they left on January 2, 1913, she made Roy's favorite bread, wrapped it and put it on the ledge of the well to keep fresh.

It didn't take long for Roy and Della to decide on a date. February 2nd was Della's choice. It would give her parents time to come from Indiana and her grandmother time to get invitations out and the reception planned and ready. Della had had other beaus. She wrote them that she was marrying Roy, and received a letter from one in return saying she had broken his heart. With the Reichards, the Colberts, the Greens, and Cranstons, Grandma Reichard suggested that a church wedding would be necessary. It was a lovely wedding. The sun shone on a bright February day, and Della was beautiful. Since the reception would last until late in the evening, Roy arranged for them to spend their wedding night in Urbana.

Early the next morning, they packed Roy's large buggy with Della's trunk, wedding presents, and other belongings, and set out for their new home on the Rose Haven Farm. It was cloudy, and Grandmother Reichard brought blankets to keep them warm, even though they were wearing winter coats.

They travelled along the State Road, and as soon as they reached Mayview it started to snow. By the time they arrived at Fithian, they were crunching through six inches. Roy turned the horses onto the dirt road that led to the farm, white with snow, bordered by fences, happy that the cold trip was almost over. But under the snow were ruts that caught the wheels, and broke one, turning the buggy over into the ditch. What a way to start a honeymoon! Roy and Della climbed out of the buggy and stood near the fallen buggy. It would be a cold walk to the house, and Roy could carry only one or two small things.

Fortunately, a neighbor driving along the road rescued them, taking them to the farm, and returned with a friend to bring all of Della's belongings. It was a memorable start for a wedding that began a long and wonderful marriage.

After Roy and Della's wedding, Alta decided to follow Roy's lead in attending the Epworth League college class. In the early spring, she met a junior in the University with a strange name—Wilfred Crouch Ropiequet. She had heard his name—he had been manager of the Star Course Concert Series, and his signs advertising "Fifteen Seats left for Galla Kirchi," and finally "Two seats left for Galla Kirchi" had all the campus laughing, wondering how fat the singer was. This year he was editor of the *Illio*, the University of Illinois year book. At the first Saturday night he was in the college class, the college students played a game challenging the men to make a lady partner laugh. Wilfred was Alta's partner, and Alta had to work very hard at not laughing as he made funny faces and tried every funny trick he knew—and that was a lot. Somehow, her self-control impressed Wilfred, and the next week he asked her for a date. He was impressive! Even though he was of medium height, he was handsome, and had a real gift of clever and thoughtful words and quotations, and full of new ideas of interesting things to do. He shared with Alta his plans to add a special humorous section to the Illio, making fun of all sorts of campus places and activities. He took a picture of University Hall, and doctored it by drawing a clothesline full of laundry across the windows, labeling it "A tenement in our midst." This time Alta laughed with him. She was not so sure she approved when he showed her a picture of her beloved Dean of Woman with the Dean of Men on "Lovers' Lane," looking back, startled as if being discovered in a compromising position. Wilfred explained that when he had taken one flash picture, and they looked back startled, he immediately took another flash picture capturing their startled expression. In May when the year book was finished, the "Sillio" section at the back was a huge success. It was a very funny addition to the traditional year book. Over the summer, Alta missed him. He lived 200 miles south in Belleville, Illinois.

The summer gave a great opportunity for Mary and the rest of the family to become friends with Della. Mary insisted on staying in the Mason house, not wanting to impose extra work on a new bride, but Della was more than happy to urge them to share meals, and seemed genuinely eager to be a part of the Green family.

In the fall of 1913, Esther accompanied Alta to the University. She was more interested in business than liberal arts. Wilfred was back for his senior year, this time working for the *Daily Illini*, the campus newspaper, as his extracurricular activity. He was bright, but not really focused on scholarship. Alta still kept her grades high, working every year for the Dean of Women. When Alta saw the headlines on the *Daily Illini*, reporting the German sinking of the Lusitania, she and everyone else were shocked. They read in bold, huge, black letters: "America Declares War!" The next day, Wilfred explained that he had been the night editor when he received the Associated Press news of the sinking of the Lusitania, and on his own decided that America was sure to enter the war in Europe at that action, so he tore out the headlines, and inserted the assumption as fact in the headline. Only two newspapers in the United States dared to publish that headline, but the next day, Congress did declare war against Germany.

There was more sad news that fall. Della, who had been delighted that she was pregnant, lost twins in a miscarriage.

By then, Wilfred and Alta were in love. He had also charmed Mary Esther. During the Easter Vacation, Alta persuaded her mother to invite him to the farm. Della insisted that he shared the bed in the sewing room with Vee, thirteen, who loved to tease. When Wilfred awoke, not too early, Saturday morning, Vee was gone, and he felt something furry in bed with him. Investigating, he found it was a dead rat. He had heard Vee had invented traps to catch the rats eating the hay in the barn. Laughing, Wilfred put the rat on Vee's chair at breakfast, saying, "You forgot your pet."

Wilfred was a city boy, but really impressed Roy and he was invited to shoot a couple of guns, from Roy's new collection, at a target he had set up. Wilfred did not confide to Roy that he had never shot a gun, but somehow he managed to hit the bulls-eye in his first shot. He never took another shot, wanting to preserve a perfect record.

Later that evening, as Wilfred and Alta observed the constellations in the clear country sky, he asked her to marry him as soon as she finished college. She agreed.

He graduated in June, and took a position as a claim adjuster in Iowa City. During the next year, he and Alta exchanged frequent letters, addressed from him: "To the Swan from the Goose."

Alta completed her education, was invited into Phi Beta Kappa, and graduated with highest honors on June 15, 1915. Wilfred came for the graduation, and stayed to marry her on June 17, saying "I can't afford two trips." With her wedding dress, Alta wore in her hair a circle of blossoms from the lemon tree. She returned with him to Iowa City, but the next year they moved to 12 Oak Terrace in Webster Grove, a suburb of St Louis, Missouri, where he began studying law at night school in Benton College of Law.

Della was adjusting nicely to farm life, but added some of her hobbies, such as singing in the choir, collecting fine pottery and china, glass, and many other lovely things. To help Roy buy the farm, she agreed, as a cash crop, to raise and help milk dairy cows. They gradually added cows until there were about twenty, each with a number instead of a name. In 1916 to get the cream for sale, they turned a hand separator, filling big cans to be picked up every morning. Della had to stop the milking for a little while when their son Robert was born that year.

In the fall of 1915, after Alta and Wilfred were married, Ruth had accompanied Esther to the University of Illinois. She was a beauty, with naturally curly light brown hair setting off a slightly round face with brilliant dark blue eyes. She had been popular with the boys in high school, and the college men eagerly asked her for dates. However, she had met at the little Methodist Church on Main street a farm boy from near the little town of Mayview, about seven miles from Urbana. Glenn H. Gordon owned an automobile—as did Roy at this time—and Ruth enjoyed being picked up in a real car for dates. Glenn was a red-head, medium height and slender, but with a real gift of words. He was helping on his father's farm, and finding the best markets for his produce and grains, but also trading horses on his own—with considerable profit. He had a great sense of humor, and many friends. Vee, still in high school, was fascinated with automobiles, and had learned from Roy during summer vacations, how to tune up and repair his car. Roy enjoyed tinkering, inventing, and repairing more than farming, and usually had one or more junk cars on the farm to repair and renew, use or sell. One time when Glenn was in the house talking with Ruth and her mother before a date, Vee opened the hood of Glenn's car and disconnected the fuel line from the carburetor. Of course, when he and Ruth drove off, the car stopped within a few blocks. Glenn, too, was familiar with car repairs, and quickly found and reattached the gas line. He and Ruth did not have to guess who had played the trick on them. It was not the first and would not be the last of Vee's tricks.

During the summer of 1916, Glenn drove several times to the Rose Haven Farm to see Ruth, and On November 29, 1917, during the Thanksgiving Vacation he and Ruth were married in the Green house on East Main Street. Ruth dropped out of school, and the couple set up housekeeping in Indiana.

Esther completed three years at the University, and took a year off to teach school at Mahomet, Illinois, not far from Champaign in western Champaign County. She came back after one year to finish her degree. Her beau at the University was Rolling Jarvis, whom she married right after graduating in 1918. They set up housekeeping in Minneapolis, Minnesota. About a year after the birth of her son Richard Rolling Jarvis in 1919, she became ill with an infection and the flu, and died.

Within a year of moving to Indiana, Glenn and Ruth returned to Illinois. They lived in a bungalow near Glenn's father's farm in Mayview, with Glenn again working with his father. In 1926, Glenn and Ruth bought the Stanner Farm a few miles from Mayview where they raised their six children.

Vivian Julius "Vee" attended the University of Illinois from 1920 to 1924. He had the privilege of being the center on the football team that featured the famous Red Grange—the "Galloping Ghost." Wilfred, Alta's husband was a "perpetual sophomore" with a great love for the U. of I. He had established a custom of returning to Urbana for the Homecoming football game every year—never missing one until he was paralyzed by a stroke in 1958. He attended the first Homecoming in the new Stadium in 1923. The Ropiequet children took pride in seeing their Uncle Vee passing the ball to the famous Red Grange. Wilfred not only brought his wife and three children to the official opening of the Memorial Stadium in 1924, but headed a caravan of about twenty cars of the St. Louis Illini Club, which he had founded, from St. Louis to Urbana. They stopped in the Mattoon square where an area had been cordoned off for cars while the Illini ate lunch. There were no heaters in the cars then, and the children shivered under blankets. That game was the most exciting ever. Red Grange made six touchdowns.

At his graduation in spring of 1924, Vee Green married Mildred Holmes. He had a career teaching science and athletics, first in high school, then as head football coach at Drake University in DesMoines.

For Christmas 1924, Mary Esther invited all her six remaining children and their families to join her in the Urbana home. Roy and Della and their three children—Robert, Roberta, and Gail—joined Alta and Wilfred with their three—Edith, Katherine, and Richard, while Ruth and Glenn, who lived near-by, came only for the day. Wilfred left right after Christmas, planning to return for his family in a week. Roy had to return to care for the animals on the farm. Richard and Martin, teens, were there. Then Mary Esther, who had never admitted to being sick, contracted scarlet fever, and all the family in the house were quarantined with her. Every day or so young men, Richard and Martin, would gather the children for a "Monkey Pile." How the little ones hated it! But they were too little to fight back. By that time, the cousins were all good friends. Robert Green—nine, was the oldest, and Edith Ropiequet was eight," but Roberta Green, Betty Gordon, and Katherine Ropiequet were all seven, and Gail Green, Glenn Gordon, Jr., and Richard Ropiequet were all five. Alta and Della managed to feed and care for all the children. "Grandma" had a young woman roomer—also quarantined—who graciously offered to crochet tiny sweaters for the girls' new Christmas dolls. Katherine asked for orange and blue for Illinois for her doll. It was a long week, but Mary Esther recovered, and the tiny sweater was a treasure for many years.

This photo of the two-family Rose Haven house was taken in April, 1958. It shows the basedment, garage, gun room, and office additions after the house was raised.

Time for the Boys

After the girls were all married, Mary Esther was delighted, in June of 1925, to return to Rose Haven Farm. Of course, the old home was now occupied by Roy and Della, who were working hard to buy the farm, promising their mother she would always have a home there. But Mary chose to live in the Mason House with Richard and Martin. She even asked Richard to plow a garden spot near the Mason House for the circular garden was now Della's. Della protested, saying, "Mother Green, only you have that magic touch that makes the vegetables and flowers flourish." Mary Esther promised to help in that garden, too, but wanted her own garden close to her house.

The last year Vee was in college, he lived in the Sigma Phi Fraternity. Richard was finishing high school in the Oakwood Township, and later he, too, lived in that fraternity. Now, they were back at Rose Haven and sixteen-year-old Martin would have a chance to know and appreciate living on the open land.

There was a sense of peace and relief. Mary loved the wide night skies sprinkled with stars, and the sweet smell of fresh-turned black earth, and wild flowers beside the roads brightening the meadows and edges of the fields. She found enough cull apples on the ground to make three quarts of applesauce. Again, on Sunday afternoons, she could wander through the woods listening for birds and finding each season's flowers or seeds. There was time to take and print the pictures of the cradle classes, and renew her friendships in the Ladies' Aid. Even in the Mason House, it was "home." And Roy was willing, even eager, to use his car to take her to church and to her meetings—or let Richard drive.

Richard offered to help Roy and Della milk the cows each morning before school, and evenings, too, and Roy insisted on paying him for his time. It was good to be saving money for college.

Della was an ideal farmer's wife. She helped with the milking, managed the garden and canning, the chickens, in addition to keeping a neat home and preparing delicious meals. And she still found time to sing and volunteer in church and town. Della's collections of glass, English china, and rocks reminded Mary of her own collection of colored stones.

In April 1924, Ruth and Glenn invited Mary to visit them to see their new home on the old Stanner Farm. Of course, Grandma Green told stories to Elizabeth, Glenn Jr., and little Mary Margaret, and rocked baby Donald. She made gingerbread, did a bit of mending, and found some cull apples in the orchard to make into applesauce. During dinner Saturday evening, she asked Elizabeth how her ear was doing. Elizabeth gave her a questioning look, and answered, "It's just fine, Grandma."

Later, when the children were in bed, Mary asked Ruth, "What did that strange look of Elizabeth's mean?"

Glenn and Ruth burst out laughing. Glenn said, "She wondered if we had told you about "Two Stuck in the Mud"? Mary looked from one to the other laughing couple. "It's quite a story. You tell her, Ruth."

Still laughing, Ruth began. "Just as we moved the last of our furniture into the Stanner house, it began to rain. It poured for two weeks, and Glenn got soaked bringing his twelve horses, a few cows, and all his machinery from his father's farm. He caught cold, and it turned into pneumonia. He was getting better when his grandfather Sadoris died. The preacher called to ask Glenn and me to sing in a quartet at his funeral. Of course, I said no. Then the day before the funeral, Sally Jennings called to say, 'Please, Ruth, reconsider. I can't find another alto anywhere.'

"I was tired of being housebound, and Glenn was dressed and lying on the davenport in the living room, feeling much better, but still weak. After some persuasion, I reluctantly agreed when Sally added, 'Mr. Morris will drive you to and from the rehearsal this afternoon, and to the funeral tomorrow. He says he will use his storm buggy and his strongest team of horses, and carry a tile shovel to knock the mud out of the spokes.' He used it, too.

"The rehearsal went well, and Glenn had no trouble with the four children. So the next day I felt all right about going to the funeral. The babies, Mary Margaret—almost two and Donald—three months, were asleep, and Elizabeth—six, and Glenn, Jr.—four, were playing quietly. Glenn was comfortable resting on the davenport. I instructed the children to stay in the house, and with Mr. Morris, drove off. Then Glenn dozed off. Elizabeth and Glenn, Jr. had been in the house for two weeks and they were eager to explore the big red barn with the two cupolas. Here was their chance. No one there could say, 'No,' and the rain had stopped. Elizabeth, making sure both she and Glenn, Jr. were warmly dressed and wore their overshoes, set out for the barn. There were four fences between the house and the barn. The first two gates were closed, so the children crawled under the barbed wire. The gate between the last field and the barnyard was open. The stock had been treading the rain-soaked barnyard until the mud was knee deep. The two children, in their overshoes, had ventured no more than twenty feet into the barnyard when they could no longer pull their feet out of the mud. Stuck!

"It took a while, struggling, before Elizabeth thought of a solution. She pulled her stocking feet out of the overshoes and her shoes, and slugged through the mud, out the open gate, and crawled under the two barbed-wire fences. Her father was still asleep. She washed the incriminating muddy stockings in the kitchen sink, and hung them, not quite clean, on a kitchen chair. Then she went quietly upstairs, changed her clothes, and finally called down through the register into the living room to wake her father and tell him of Junior's plight. He pulled himself up, put on his wraps and boots and rescued Glenn Jr., standing helpless, crying pitifully. Then, with difficulty, he pulled Elizabeth's overshoes out of the mud. All were clean, quiet, and peaceful when I got home, the babies still asleep."

"I'll bet those children got a real scolding!" Grandma Green said.

"They really didn't need it. They had learned a lesson, and were most repentant. But that's not the end of the story. About a week later, Elizabeth came downstairs for breakfast complaining of her ear hurting. It was red and swollen around a dark red scratch. Elizabeth had torn it on the barbed wire as she crawled under it, but didn't think it was worth mentioning. The doctor gave an immediate shot, and prescribed hot packs continuously, renewed every twenty minutes, for at least 24 hours, with no time out for sleep. The ear got worse, swelling the whole side of her face, but it did heal in about a week. She was so ashamed that she didn't want me to tell the story to you."

"I'll not tell her that I know," Grandma Green promised. However, in December 1957, Ruth wrote the whole story beautifully as a Christmas present for her children.

Back in Urbana

Richard graduated from the Oakwood High school, and at the University of Illinois, pledged to Sigma Phi, and lived there his freshman year. He took wrestling as his physical education course, and became interested in it as a sport. But in 1925, when Martin was ready for college, Mary moved back into the Urbana house. This time, with no babies to care for, she found a job at Didson's Greenhouse on East Main Street, just a short walk from her house. It was sheer joy for her to be working with plants again.

Family was a vital part of Mary Esther's life. Week-ends on the farm with Roy and Della, or Sunday afternoons with Ruth and Glenn and their children were frequent. She welcomed Alta and Wilfred, with their three children, every other Christmas in Urbana, and frequently for summer vacations in the Mason House. She kept in contact with Lucy and Wilbert, her mother, Artemissa Cranston, and her sister Clara Jeanette. Grace, too. Gibson City was close, and even brother Leslie and his wife moved to Oakwood, Illinois, establishing his law practice in Danville, about ten miles east. Emma Carpenter, Lincoln's sister, after the death of her blacksmith husband, lived on the outskirts of Oakwood near Lucy and Wilbert's farm.

Richard decided he did want to be a farmer, but also was interested in mathematics and science. His early interest in wrestling earned him an "I" as an extra-curricular activity, and Martin followed in his pathway, also earning an "I" in wrestling, but majoring in business instead of agriculture.

The Happiest Years

When Richard graduated from the University in 1928, his Uncle Wilbert retired from farming and moved in to the Victorian house in Oakwood that he had designed and had built. He offered to rent Richard his farm on the outskirts of Oakwood. It was a good opportunity, and accepting it, Richard asked his mother if she would like to come live there and keep house for him. For Mary, it was a chance to be useful and back on the land with her Oakwood family and friends. Martin, who had also pledged Sigma Phi, could live there his senior year. She sold the Urbana house and moved into Wilbert and Lucy's farm house. When Martin graduated in 1929, he found a job in East St. Louis, Illinois, and stayed with his sister Alta and her family for a year. Then he received a position with the Bell Telephone Company, married his sweetheart Madelyn, and moved to Chicago.

The old Wilbert Green home on the north edge of Oakwood was a typical farm home, with a kitchen large enough for a big dining table, a dining room used for family, a parlor on the first floor, and three bedrooms upstairs. There was electricity and running water, luxuries not yet in the Mason House. Roy had set up a generator to electrify the Rose Haven Farm house, and pump water into the kitchen, but left the Mason house as it was. Mary placed her lemon and orange trees near the living room window, and decorated window sills with her seedling flowers in their make-do pots.

Richard was an innovative farmer, trying new kinds of crops, such as Christmas trees, or rose bushes as fence substitutes. The 1930's were difficult years for farmers. Droughts, chinch bugs, and the depression made farming a challenge, but Richard managed to keep going. He also wrestled in matches all around the neighboring towns on occasional Saturdays to earn extra money. While he rested in mid-days, he enjoyed listening to base ball games on his radio. During winter days of limited work, Richard carved interesting pieces of wood into birds or other animals, giving them away to his visitors.

With no children to care for except visiting grandchildren, Mary, for the first time in her life, had time for her own interests. The Oakwood Methodist Church, just a few blocks from the farm, claimed much of her time. In addition to the pictures of the cradle classes, she became Superintendent of the Sunday school, and active in Ladies' Aid. She gathered a group to share their poetry, remembering her pleasure sharing poems in Antioch College, and in the early days of her marriage. Then the church asked her to be their historian in a project of gathering the history of Oakwood. Mary searched through the records of Oakwood and Vermillion County, libraries, and newspaper files, finding many statistics, but most rewarding were her interviews with the earliest settlers and their descendants. Those yielded not only history as far back as the original Indians, but also many humorous and revealing anecdotes. Five members of the Sunday School class, with her help, worked the material into an accurate and interesting *History of Oakwood, 1820 to 1930*.

In her memoirs, Mary Esther Cranston Green wrote, "These

years on the farm at the outskirts of Oakwood were the happiest years of my life." She had her garden, her lemon and orange trees, and flowers all over her house. But, best of all, she had free time—lots of it. She started biennial family reunions, sometimes at the Rose Haven Farm, with Della's encouragement, and sometimes in Oakwood. How the cousins of each generation enjoyed getting to know each other—even the crowding three in a bed! One summer the Ropiequet and Gordon children playing together found a huge roller-tank, with circular openings on each end about 12" in diameter. Six of them pushed their way through the circular holes, and standing up on the inside, started walking together to roll the big tank across the yard. It was fun! But when they tired of the sport and pushed their way out of the tank, I—Katherine, who was huskier than the others, couldn't push myself out. Mother and Grandma Green came to the rescue, and finally found a way to twist shoulders first, then hips, to crowd through the 12" hole.

Grandma Green was always dependable in solving problems, and grandchildren could count on her to have some gingerbread on the table. They also enjoyed twisting their heads and stretching or stooping to read the comic papers used as wallpaper in her storeroom off the kitchen, or looking up to identify the 8x10 pictures of birds making a border around the dining room ceiling. These were taken down every January, and added one by one as birds were sighted on walks through the woods or in yard or field. The Green children and grandchildren could recognize many, many birds and their calls, and many wildflowers, too. Grandma Green was always an unsuspected teacher with surprising bits of knowledge for her grandchildren. They enjoyed using the apple peeler. She shared a folk myth that if a young lady could peel an apple with the skin still in one piece, she could toss it on the ground. If it fell in the shape of a letter, it was the first letter in the name of the man she would marry.

In 1937, Mary and Richard shared a trip to Colorado with daughter Alta and Wilfred Ropiequet and two of their children. In the mountain meadows, Mary Green picked almost 200 wildflowers, pressing them in catalogs. Later, she identified most of them, blueprinting the most interesting, painting them in watercolors, and giving copies to Alta and her daughter Katherine, all labeled. These blueprints are now in a scrapbook at her great-grandson Roger's house.

Oakwood and Fithian also had free movies on Saturday nights in the summer, when all the shops were open for business. The movies were usually old, old cowboy movies, and often the film broke, but the audience would cheer and boo, and enjoy every moment. Frequent intermissions gave the shopkeepers their turn, too, and the children time to play. Everybody knew Mary, and she would introduce her grandchildren with pride.

Richard Green was always interesting. Talented in calligraphy, he also taught his nieces to print with shadow letters. He confessed that when he rested his horses at the end of a row of plowing, he would read or work Calculus problems in his head. Later, he was the first one in Vermillion County to have a gasoline powered tractor and corn-picker. He sometimes let the little nephews ride with him on the tractor. He also pondered the nature of light, confident that light not only came in waves with measurable wave-lengths, but also that it consisted of particles. He put together a simple but accurate experiment to prove his theory. Starting with a shoe box, carefully sealed, with a camera, lens-free, but with film, he placed it in a window bright with sunlight, made a pinhole to let light enter, and took color pictures of the patterns of light as it came through the pinhole and various filters. He wrote a scholarly study of the geometric patterns shown on his photographic slides, asserting that they proved that light did have particles. The geometric patterns on the slides are beautiful, basically two axes with concentric circles of various colors, often spreading far out with sparkling dashes of bright red or another color. These slides are now in the possession of the Physics Department of the University of Illinois, and they made an interesting oil painting.

The years in Oakwood with Richard also gave Mary Esther freedom to grow intellectually. This was the time for the next generation, too. Not only in the biennial family reunions on the Rose Haven Farm or at the Wilbert Green farm, but on frequent visits of her children's families, Mary Esther Cranston Green served as hostess, story teller, teacher, and creator of innovative play things. If asked about a rare five-petalled lavender flower growing in a tin can on her window sill, she could give the botanic gendre, name of Platicodium, and characteristics. She knew the names and habitats of all the birds pictured in the circle around the dining room ceiling. She was willing to teach her granddaughters how to cut the strands from old bathrobes, pants, and wool shirts, and braid them in three or seven strands and curl the braided strips into rugs as she had done with her own daughters. When she made their favorite gingerbread or cookies, she let them lick the cookie bowl. It was fun to use the apple peeler, too, and to crank the shaft on the non-automatic washing machine in the side yard.

When the city granddaughters were ironing with the stove-heated iron, she would teach them to "...iron slowly. It conserves the heat of the iron and your energy,"

Lucy and Wilbert, retired, in their large and beautiful Victorian house with towers and ginger-bread trim in the middle of Oakwood, were now active in the social life of the town. Lucy became interested in genealogy, and traced her ancestry back to John Alden and Priscilla of the early pilgrims. She joined the "Daughters of the Revolution," and morphed from a farmer's wife to a "lady." Mary was still her unpretentious self, Superintendent of the Sunday school, taking pictures of the cradle class, keeping house for a farmer, active in Ladies' Aid, and historian for "Oakwood 1820-1930," class, sharing her poetry, writing a newspaper article about the values and pleasures of a pond, and praying and praising her Lord. Their paths didn't meet very often, but she, Wilbert and their four girls did enjoy the family reunions and their relatives.

The Rose Have Farm was still the magnet that held the entire Cranston, Green, Reichard, and Colbert families together during summer vacations. Roy was inventive and capable. Early in their marriage, probably 1924-5, he had the family house raised and put in a basement beneath it, with plumbing—a real toilet on a block of concrete, a furnace with heat flowing up through a 6' x 6' grate, shelves for jars and jars of canned goods, a drain in the floor, and space for parking his car—down a steep slope as it was seldom used. Of course, the water system required an electric pump, and that necessitated a generator and called for electrification of the house. He installed ceiling lights in each room, with pull-chains. The children sometimes surreptitiously pulled these for fun. As a 5-year-old, Elizabeth Gordon kept hoping Aunt Della wouldn't ask her to go into that dark basement to get a can of fruit.

With the house up high, he extended it further beyond the "new kitchen" to add a gun room half-way up the back stairs. He had a fabulous collection of guns—all kinds. He never bothered to put steps up to the front door, for everyone used either the side door or the back one. He built a porch off the kitchen and dining room, and later enclosed it with windows. It became the preferred dining area. Heat rose into the house through the huge grate, a wonderful place to stand on cold days absorbing the welcome warmth. He even had a grate put in the floor of the back seat of his car to let the engine heat warm the car. His shop was crammed with many, many tools and always had the right nail, screw, glue, wood or metal or part for any repair or innovative device. Neighbors found it handy, too, and were always welcome to take what they needed. More interested in gadgets than farming, Roy usually had one or two junk cars sitting around to be repaired and then used.

Roy was generous—even rescuing the Ropiequet family after an automobile accident just east of Decatur, Illinois. With Wilfred in the hospital with a head injury, he picked up his sister Alta, her father-in-law, and her daughter, and drove them to Urbana to the stadium to attend the Homecoming game. Despite protests, Wilfred checked himself out of the hospital and hitch-hiked, with bandaged head, to the stadium to join them in the stands.

Della was truly amazing. She seemed interested and knowledgeable about everything, and was able to handle everything without seeming harassed. She welcomed everybody's help with meals—if they were quick enough. She played the piano, taught her daughter to play beautifully, continued to sing solos and with the choir, was active in social groups, and raised three children, and she always seemed to have time to share her knowledge about her collections. She was responsible for offering their farm as a place for the Danville College astronomy club to build their little observatory with a telescope to study the stars, away from town lights. The blackboard on the closed-in porch always had some interesting saying on it, as well as notes.

And every family was always welcome, without an invitation.

During the years 1928-1938, Mary kept house for Richard and did a lot of writing—getting some of it published in the local papers. A number of her poems appeared in the *Oakwood newspaper*—a short-lived venture, the history of Oakwood, of course, and various articles. But more than that, she was friend, teacher, mentor, and helper to dozens of family members and hundreds of neighbors. She was free to be herself with time to invest as she pleased.

In 1938, Richard surprised her by announcing he was marrying Marian Rutherford. He had been seeing her often, finding her very interesting and challenging—for their political views were direct opposites. Mary and Richard were both surprised when Mary's sister Lucy told them she wanted them to move out of her and Wilbert's farm house. Later, a friend told Mary in confidence that she thought Lucy was jealous of her. Mary found that hard to believe. Lucy was so active in organizations, especially the Daughters of the Revolution, had four fine married daughters and delightful grandchildren—even though they didn't visit often—and was so much a lady. Mary couldn't imagine Lucy could be jealous of ordinary Mary Cranston Green, but Mary would have to find another place to live.

From left: Mary Cranston Green, Della Reichard Green, and unknown woman and boy.

The pond today, looking much as it did when Mary and Lincoln Green lived there, except for the sign in the distance.

Part V

Back on Rose Haven Farm

Spreading and Thriving

Marian and Richard chose to have a simple wedding in the church parlor with just the local relatives attending. During the small reception, Roy sat down next to his mother and said, "Now that all your children are married and doing well, it's finally time for you to come home to Rose Haven Farm. We've been saving that room for you."

Before Mary could say anything, Della was there giving her a hug. "Mother Green, I can hardly wait until you come back to your real home. I told Roy to be sure you don't try to go off somewhere else to live. Your garden needs you, and I'll enjoy your company."

Mary didn't want to be a burden on anyone, but it would be good to be living on that farm again. She moved into the house Lincoln had built for them in 1891. It had been a happy home. She took a moment to remember Lincoln, his love and laughter, the little sorghum factory, the roses, her circular garden. How she missed Lincoln! But with God's help she had raised and educated her children. They didn't need her any more. Yes, she should be with family. She took Roy's hand in hers, and Della's in her other one, saying, "Thank you for making me welcome. It is the best place for me now. I hope I can be a real help to you both, and not a burden."

With a lighter heart, Mary gave Marian a warm welcome into the Green family. She congratulated Richard on his wise choice of a mate, wishing them both God's blessings, in the farm Richard had purchased in Chebanse, Illinois.

In a few days Mary had disposed of her extra furniture and was settled with her personal belongings: sewing machine, knitting needles, and crochet hooks in the front bedroom of her old home in Rose Haven Farm. She did not intend to be idle. From her windows she could see the road, once lined with rose bushes, and the pond. Della had insisted the lemon and orange tree come with her. Early the next morning, she was in the garden, making plans.

Mary was proud of each of her remaining six children, determined to keep in touch with all of them. It had meant so much to her that her parents, and Lincoln's too, had been loving and caring. And in the years that followed, she found that her children and grandchildren also treasured her.

Della moved so fast with the housework and cooking that Mary, still strong at 71, had to hurry to help. They soon formed a partnership, with Mary helping set the table, getting food on the table, and washing the dishes. Della was grateful for more time for her hobbies.

As Roy and his sons helped with the hard work of the garden, Mary supervised and tended her plants. Gardening was Mary's joy. She still was Superintendent of the Sunday school, and kept up her pictures of the cradle class, and with Della met with the Ladies' Aid. After keeping in touch with letters with all her children, there was still time enough to make her aprons from flour sacks, do the mending for active farm workers, and make her Afghans and braided rugs. She refused to sit idly in a rocking chair. "Rest is a change of occupation," and "Satan finds things for idle hands to do," were welcome sayings. She was still writing. She kept up with news, local and national, and sent letters, poems, and articles to the newspapers.

With her faith, her philosophy and her talents, she was a welcome visitor at the homes of each of her children. The grandchildren all loved and respected her. Although she sought mending and other tasks to keep her hands busy, she loved the children, told them stories, helped them with their broken toys, and planned projects with them. Unless asked, she seldom gave advice. She also shared her recipe for raising the seven children and getting them all through college—except Ruth, who quit to get married: "Waste not, want not," "Make it do, use it up, wear it out," "It's good enough," and in discipline, "Ask yourself, 'Is it really important'—if it is, insist. If not, let it go."

For a while after he graduated, Robert, eldest of Roy and Della's three children, stayed on the farm, but when he met his cousin Dorothy Pointer in Tennessee on a visit to his uncle Stephen and aunt Emma, he fell in love, and asked her to marry him. Although he had graduated from the U of I in Ceramic Engineering, he decided to go into Contracting. They lived for a few years in the Oakwood area, then moved to Peoria. Roberta worked for a while as a secretary before marrying Grant Mathis, moving to Rantoul, near Urbana. Gail married Dolores, his high school sweetheart, and decided to make his career joining his dad Roy, in working Rose Haven Farm.

Alta and Wilfred, who liked to drive, came to the farm with their family on alternate Christmases, summer vacations, and often brought Mary home to stay with them in the St. Louis area. Alta used to say, and she probably heard it from her mother, "A tear is but the exigency of the moment, but a patch is premeditated poverty." However, both of them believed in mending and patching, to "make do" with clothes longer. She and Alta designed and made an Afghan from grandson Richard's Navy uniform, and another from Alta's discarded grey wool coat. They have become heirlooms. Both are beautiful with added crocheted roses and leaves, and joined and edged with crocheted yarn. Alta appreciated her mother's help as she bought cherries, peaches and berries by the bushel to can for winter desserts. With a brand new disposal, they ground pits from a bushel of cherries. Noisy!

Ruth and Glenn had six children, Elizabeth, Glenn Jr., Mary Margaret, Donald, and the youngest—twin girls, Jean and Janette. Mary was a big help to all their family, an innovative fix-it specialist. Ruth, always busy, was cheerful and seemed to have no trouble keeping six children, house, and chores under control. She once said children were easier to handle in even numbers than odd. Glenn concocted a way to have water pumped from their well by a big windmill. He was a good farmer and gifted at trading horses. All the family appreciated their collie Rover, who guarded the twins carefully, one time pushing them from the road to the ditch as a car approached too fast. Ruth, like her mother, kept her hands busy. She sewed clothes for their children, made quilts in her spare time, or pillows out of goose down. Those made greatly appreciated wedding gifts. Her heart was as big as all outdoors.

Vee and Mildred were raising two boys. Mary wondered why, when he had expressed dislike of his name—Vivian Julius, he named his sons Christian and Wilfred Martin. Mildred "Mid" was fastidious, wearing a white uniform around the house, and keeping everything sanitary. She was a very good cook, specializing in pheasant or venison, whatever her hunter husband shot. Vee had a collection of hub caps. The street in front of their home in the suburbs of DesMoines, Iowa, was good at knocking off the hubcaps. Vee kept them for drivers who might return seeking lost items, but few picked them up. Vee was by then coaching the Drake football team. He was a good coach and story-teller.

Richard, known to his friends as Dick and his wife Marian raised Richard, Jr. and Nancy on their Chebanse Farm. Dick became active in political affairs in nearby Kankakee, and was highly respected, named "Farmer of the Year," and served as Farm Supervisor in Kankakee. His son when he grew up, went on to get his Ph.D in physics, and worked on government space program projects. Martin and Madelyn lived in the Chicago area, where he worked for the Bell Telephone Company. Their children were Valerie and Martin Jr. The slight limp never seemed to bother Martin. He enjoyed golf and other activities.

Rolling Jarvis remarried a few years after Esther died and soon after Richard Rolling Jarvis was born. Richard came to some of the family reunions, and visited a few of his aunts and uncles. As a teen cousin, he was noteworthy for his skills with the sword, and his fondness for Cyrano de Bergerac. On his visit to the Ropiequets, Edith, getting tired of hearing about Cyrano, started calling him Cyanide, and he responded by calling her Poison Ivy. On a later visit to the farm, early in the morning he asked, "Where do I get hot water to shave?" The answer, to his surprise, was, "Turn on the faucet." Uncle Roy had extended the plumbing to the bathroom, too.

With Roy and Della's gracious encouragement, Mary continued welcoming her children and grandchildren for visits, and when invited, visiting them. She observed the many activities of the children as they enjoyed the pond, and thought about the great advantages to them all of having a pond, fed by underground water, always clear and available.

One year, after the grandchildren were mostly married and away, Roy let the hogs enjoy the pond, but they sure did mess it up. One visitor unknowingly dipped in the pond for a swim. It was a messy disaster. The next year the hogs were banished, and Roy restored the pond to its pristine splendor. Like Mary, all the visiting family appreciated the positive influence and pleasures of the pond.

Mary Cranston Green. Happy dinner with family.

Mary, Alta, Edith and Katherine "Kit", 1937.

Planting Seeds of Love, Help and Wisdom

During these years of visits to and visits from her children and grandchildren, Mary Esther Cranston Green probably influenced for the good multitudes of people, setting the example of unselfish love, directed use of talents and time, and wisdom to share when appropriate, but never forced on anyone. Always, though privately, she was praying for all her loved ones. Calm and unruffled, she was ready to help, or share her knowledge of botany and geology, housekeeping and farming, child-raising, and making-do." But often she was unobtrusively minding her own business and observing, with her hands busy. She was still active in the church and community. She always enjoyed trips and new experiences with her children and their children, too.

In 1942, during World War II, many of Mary's children and grandchildren joined her and Roy and Della for Christmas. A number of the grandsons were in the service, including Robert Green, Glenn Gordon Jr., and Richard Lincoln Ropiequet. Richard, training in the Navy in Chicago, came to the Rose Haven Farm for Christmas 1943, to be with his parents and his relatives for a few days. He must have inherited some of the desire to help from his grandmother, for when he tried to play the piano in the living room, he discovered it was badly out of tune. He spent his whole three days tuning the piano. Mary was fascinated with the tuning process, and expressed her delight in his "concert" on the tuned piano. Sadly, Richard had to return to his unit on Christmas day, so his family, Wilfred, Alta, and Katherine, ate Christmas dinner in the crude Danville, Illinois, Railroad Station, the only restaurant open on Christmas Day. But they did treasure Christmas holidays with Grandma and their relatives. Edith, though, was in California with her husband Stuart Potter and their two children.

A Great-Grandmother
With Loving Heart and Busy Hands

Mary enjoyed the centennial parade at Ft. Riley in 1952 with Lloyd J. and Katherine Ropiequet Inman, appreciating the chair Lloyd had brought for her, sharing the enthusiasm of their three young boys sitting on the curb. As they watched the covered wagons pull by, the military couples dressed in pioneer clothes, and the marching horseback soldiers and bands, Grandma Green told the three boys about her moving by covered wagon when she was nine years old, reading the book, *Chinese Fairy Tales,* she had received for her ninth birthday. Lloyd really appreciated her, and gave Grandma Green credit for Katherine's willingness to marry a poor farm boy who worked his way through college with four jobs. She had asked Katherine once, having met Lloyd several times while visiting the Ropiequet family, "What are you looking for, platinum? Lloyd is pure gold." She was right.

Later, in 1958, Alta and Wilfred took Mary to visit Captain Lloyd and Katherine Inman and their boys in Springfield, Virginia. She commented that she had never been so close to the coast before. Wilfred and Lloyd immediately planned a picnic on the shore of the

Atlantic with her, Alta, Katherine, and the three boys crowded in his Buick. She was delighted with the view of the great Atlantic "Although not much different from Lake Michigan," she said. She waded in the shallow water, and on the beach, picked up shells and interesting pebbles with the three boys and Alta, who enjoyed collecting shells and rocks, too. She could identify the rocks, and investigated the identities of the shells. Lloyd took them to the mall, museums and Azalea Gardens in Washington D.C., too. She admired the azaleas, absorbed the science in the Space Museum with its planes and movies. What a wide range of interests she had! And all the mending got done, too.

Granddaughter Elizabeth and her husband Louis Wood remember Mary's visit at their home, reminding her of the time she and Glenn Jr. were "Stuck in the Mud." She commented that times of trouble become times of fun and laughter when softened by memory. On that visit, Elizabeth and Louis were awakened by a loud bang. They rushed into the guest room to find their grandmother Green lying on the floor on a collapsed mattress. The slats had fallen out of the bed frame. Louis reached to help her up, but she said calmly, "Don't bother. I'll just sleep here until morning." Elizabeth added as she told the story, "I really did love Grandma Green!"

Mary kept close to Ruth's family as they moved from the farm to Urbana in 1943. Glenn found it easy to adapt his horse-trading skills to selling real estate. Mary Margaret remembered how much she enjoyed living at home in Urbana during her last year at the University of Illinois. During World War II, Ruth often invited soldiers stationed at Chanute Field near Urbana for dinner. They became friends, and frequently wrote in appreciation and friendship from their overseas duties. Ruth kept a big bundle of these letters.

Just after Martin graduated from U of I, before he was married, he came to stay with Wilfred and his sister Alta while he worked for Aluminum Ore Co. in East St. Louis, Illinois. During that year, Wilfred brought Mary down for a visit. She so enjoyed the Municipal Opera and Forrest Park, especially the Jewel Box, a huge greenhouse full of plants and flowers. The trips into the Ozarks with the red bud and dogwood trees in bloom, and wild flowers in the hilly woods of Missouri were educational for the grandchildren and a delight to her. Although the genres of the flowers were new to her, she could identify them. She was with the Ropiequets again for Christmas in 1956 in their new home in Collinsville, Illinois, when all three of Alta and Wilfred's children and all her grandchildren were there. She passed the test of being a fascinating and helpful Great-grandmother, too.

Della and Roy continued the biennial family reunions. These were times for the grandchildren to meet their cousins and second cousins, aunts and uncles, and even great aunts and uncles. Mary kept in contact with all her sisters and brothers and their mates as long as they lived.

Rose Haven Farm became a refuge for Vee Green. He and Mildred had decided to divorce in 1956, and since he had retired from coaching, he was without a home or a job. He took a position selling funds for an investment company, and then married a nurse he had met in Iowa—Lois. They bought a trailer home, but needed a place to keep it. Again, Roy and Della, with approval of Mother Green, offered to let them live in the trailer on Rose Haven farm until they decided where to settle. It was months before they found a home in Urbana, Illinois, and bought an apartment building as an investment. In 1969, Vee died. Lois, from Iowa, had the Green family with all their generous love, as friends, and family, loving her and her three small children. Ruth in Urbana, too, was a good friend. There is such an advantage to being part of a loving family of many generations.

Just before Christmas 1967, Lloyd Inman got orders to Vietnam, and he and Katherine decided that Katherine should rent a home in Urbana for the year to be near all three of her boys, two already in the University and one a senior in High School, due for college in September 1968. Uncle Glenn found a house for them not far from campus, too small to hold all her furniture, but it was so much better for Katherine to be near her three sons, her relatives, Grandma Green, Ruth and Glenn, and Lois and her three children. Katherine and Lois became fast friends, both of them missing their husbands. Katherine was amazed at how proficient Lois was in taking care of two apartment buildings, doing almost all of the repair and renovations by herself, managing the renting and business, her home and children.

The Cranston and Green families had gravitated toward Oakwood. Clara Jeanette and her boys stayed in Gibson City after Artemissa died, and Stephen and his family, after Roy took over farming Rose Haven Farm, were in Arkansas. Emma Carpenter, Lincoln's sister, was also in Oakwood. Leslie, Mary's brother and his family moved to Oakwood, with a law practice in Danville, and Lucy and Wilbert were in their Victorian home in Oakwood. Ruth and Glenn, in Urbana, were about thirty miles from the farm, and Lois also stayed in Urbana. Richard and Marian in Chebanse were within a few hours driving distance from the Farm, and even Chicago was not too far for Martin and Madelyn to visit the farm. Mary kept the family close. The Rose Haven Farm became the anchor, the magnet that held them together. That was also true for the Reichard and Colbert families related to Della. Della's father Ves came to work at the farm for a short time, and he and Flavia settled in Muncie, just a few miles from Rose Haven Farm. One of Alta's grandsons also married a Colbert, and settled in Champaign, as did Glenn Jr. and Loraine. Mary Cranston Green's year at the University of Illinois, and her seven Illini children started a tradition at the University of Illinois. Five generations: Mary Cranston, all seven of her children, and Alta, her three children, and two grandchildren have graduated from that university since Mary Cranston attended the first class that admitted women. Also, Robert, Mary Margaret, Glenn Jr., Donald, and probably more of Mary C. Green's grandchildren graduated from the University of Illinois. Many more Illini were added by marriage.

In 1957 Wilfred Ropiequet, who, with Alta's help, had been practicing law from a wheelchair for seven years, had another stroke. This one completely disabling him. When Lloyd and Katherine visited him and Alta in their home in Collinsville, Illinois, Lloyd realized that his mother-in-law Alta, now 74, could not handle Wilfred by herself, and arranged for them to come to live in Springfield, Virginia, with them. It was working out well, when, in December 1959, Wilfred insisted he wanted to go home. Major Inman had just received orders to Amphibious Group 4 in Norfolk. Wilfred did not want to move there. He reiterated that he wanted to go home! Their Collinsville house was rented. Alta had a problem. Della Green, and Gail and Dolores, with eager consent from Mary Esther, graciously offered to let Alta and bed-ridden Wilfred stay at the Rose Haven Farm until they could move back to their Collinsville home. They were family! With her furniture in a trailer and Wilfred lying on the back seat, Katherine drove her parents from Virginia to the farm in their car, and flew back to Virginia to move her family to Norfolk in time for Christmas. Roy and Della arranged a bed for Wilfred in the dining room, near the big heat register. They all helped Alta care for him, but before their house was available, Wilfred died.

Alta did return to the Collinsville house later that year, but found it lonely and difficult. When Lloyd, in 1963, received orders to serve in Europe, he invited Alta to move to Heidelberg, Germany, with them. She was hesitant, but eager to see Europe, and to be with family without the responsibilities of caring for a home. She was concerned about missing her mother and family, but Lloyd persuaded her to join them, and the Army helped by declaring her a dependent. Heidelberg was lovely, and Alta joined the "Heidelberg Mothers" for luncheons and tours of Spain and Italy. But when she received word in 1965 that her mother had died, she was heartbroken that she had not been there. Della sent her newspapers reviews of her life and influence. Although it was too late to say goodbye to her mother, Alta returned to Illinois. Roy had died, and Della was failing a little. Gail and Dolores, living in the home they had built near the old house, invited Alta to come to the farm, her childhood home, to keep Della company, and watch over her while he was in the fields. Mary had instilled in her children her love of family. Alta stayed on the Rose Haven Farm, in the house where she was born, until Della died.

Although all of Lincoln and Mary's children are gone, and most of the grandchildren have passed on, the influence of that wise and wonderful woman is still sustaining and inspiring the following generations. Her unwavering faith, her love of education, dedication to being useful and keeping busy, the ingenuity in solving problems, her appreciation of every person for who he is, and her loving serenity are evident in her progeny.

Epilogue—Heritage

The Cousins Reunion

The Rose Haven Farm had welcomed many relatives and guests, but Gail and Dolores missed the larger family reunions where cousins could share memories. There were a lot of Greens with loving memories of their grandmother Green and Della Reichard Green. Dolores and Gail decided to invite all the living children and next generation cousins to a reunion at the Farm on June 6, 1971.

They came from near and far, from Urbana, Chebanse, and Chicago, Illinois, Indianapolis, and even California! A few of Lincoln and Mary's children, or their mates, proved they were still alive and well: Alta Ropiequet, Ruth and Glenn Gordon, Lois Green—widow of Vee, Richard and Marian Green and their wives were there. The next generation, the cousins, were represented by Roberta and Gail, of course, with Dolores, Edith Ropiequet Dietrich, Lois and Vee's three children, Douglas, Bonnie and Sally. Mary Esther's sister Grace A. DeSold, born in 1891, managed to make the trip. Also there were Raymond Green, born in 1891, and his wife Marian H. Green. He was the son of the Raymond Green who had lived across the road of the Rose Haven Farm in 1891.

Other relatives who had enjoyed visits to the farm and the family reunions accepted the invitation, too. Names familiar in the family tree: Edith Cranston (b. 1913, daughter of Stephen), Mary and Earl Waggoner (b. December of 1894, son of Clara Jeanette), Bernice Cranston Burgess (daughter of Lucy), and Dale Burgess, Jean Cranston (Leslie's son), and his wife Louise, Mary C. Cranston (b. 1906, probably Leslie's daughter), and Addie Green Burns.

There were letters from some who could not come, updating addresses. Even this gathering of two generations expressed the unity of family over many years. And the Rose Haven Farm contributed to shared memories.

A very prim Mary Esther Cranston Green, 1958.

Centennial Celebration

In 1991 or '92, four Greens, Roy's son Gail and his wife Dolores, their son Kevin and his wife Sue, and their daughter Kristine and her husband, held a centennial celebration of the Rose Haven Farm. About four hundred relatives, friends and neighbors shared fun, food, and memories, and honored Mary C. Green during the two-day Centennial Celebration. *The News Gazette*, featured the event with story and pictures.

Dolores had asked with the invitation, for family members who had spent vacations on the farm to contribute notes of their memories to share with those who celebrated together. To restore the Rose Haven Farm closer to its original condition, even with the old house gone, Gail and Dolores, with Kevin and Sue and Kristine repaired and renewed the old corn crib and barn that Roy had built. They put a lot of thought and effort into managing the large crowd expected, and making sure the visit would be rewarding for all. Dolores wrote describing the plans and preparation:

All of us out at the farm "had a whale of a lot of hard work to do getting everything ready for such a big bash, and hadn't the vaguest idea how many might come." They planned activities for the children or anyone: not only swimming in the pond, but croquet, trampoline, horseshoes, and volley-ball, "The biggest job was clearing the largest machine shed—100' x 150' or so, of equipment, cleaning up as much as that type of place could be. We scrubbed the walls, and then painted the floor just two days before the celebration. It would be an alternative gathering place in case of rain. July had been the wettest ever, more in that one month than in the previous three months. What could we do if it rained on the picnics?"

They added makeshift tables and benches—assembled planks on stands. Feeding such an uncertain number for two days was a challenge. Dolores planned to serve everyone barbequed meat, hamburger or hot dog sandwiches, and ask guests to bring covered dishes. She would provide ice tea, and maybe lemonade, and maybe some home-made ice cream—but for so big a crowd that would be impractical. The people would bring cake and pies.

Delores assigned herself the task of making posters to show the history of the farm in the big shed. Scrapbooks made long ago were gone, so she sorted through a totally unorganized box of old tin-types to find what she needed to make some sense out of posters. She wrote to Katherine Inman afterwards: "I did about eight posters of the different generations, and one of old farm machinery and equipment, one of old cars, and various kinds of transportation, etc. Then I wrote something about each generation. Those, and letters from the various cousins about what they remembered about the farm, were put in various notebook folders and on display for anyone to read about that cared to. I included the stories you sent, very well written, and sounded like the true facts to me, good reading."

One of the letters, from Harold Colbert, nephew of Della and

Roy, gave a picture of some of the complications in a harvest on Rose Haven Farm:

One Harvest season, Robert Green and Harold Colbert were water boys for the harvesters. They carried water from the house to the workers in the field in an old Nash Sedan, one of the cars Roy had rescued from the dump. It was a full-time job, for the workers in the summer heat were always thirsty. On one return trip, the Nash slipped from the muddy road to the ditch. Robert simply gunned the motor, and drove the rest of the way to the house in the ditch, splattering mud all over.

"On another harvesting season, the tractor—attached by a long belt to the threshing machine, caught fire, setting the stubble burning. Uncle Roy raced back to the house to get another tractor and a plow, and came back to plow around the fire, through fences and all, and even through fire, to keep it from spreading and destroying machinery, crops, and endangering the threshers. Then he went to his shop, found the proper parts, and repaired the burnt out thresher. Threshing proceeded. His courage and mechanical skill left a lasting impression on this nephew."

A letter from Don Colbert, nephew of Della Reichard Green, gives a good example of the many letters received from all the visiting nephews, nieces and other relatives who benefitted from vacations on Rose Haven Farm.

"1932-1992: The Green Farm revisited—

"I remember the farm of Uncle Roy Green and Aunt Della Reichard Green opened wide the eyes of many nephews and nieces. The city kids learned about livestock, tractors, bailers, soy beans, cooking farm-style—a million things including fun times and hard, hard work.

"Sometimes the trip began with a ride on the Urbana-to-

Danville Interurban street-car. The motorman let me off at the gravel road that leads to the farm house. I could walk the rest of the way. Now we jump off of I-74—what a change! I was blessed with an invitation several summers to stay a few days, often with my cousins Jerry Reichard and David Warren Reichard—that's when Aunt Della's patience was tried! Trouble followed us several times, as when we left the gate open to a corn field, and the cattle enjoyed their green heaven. Or when Jerry and I went swimming in the pond when it was a hog lot—a real no, no!

"I remember:

"Aunt Della starting her kitchen stove fire with dried corn cobs.

"Uncle Roy working on his three "twin city" tractors that had steel cleat wheels.

"Aunt Della separating the cream from the cow barn on her fascinating, whirring cream separator.

"Carrying water to the threshers—out by the huge chaff pile and wondering how the leather belt stayed on the pulleys on the threshing machine and the power tractor anchored 30 feet away.

"Uncle Roy boiling the sorghum cane forever and ever—then running it into the metal gallon cans to be sold as 'Green Farm Sorghum'—umm, good!

"Eating fried chicken, mountains of mashed potatoes, green beans, and apple pie on the farm house porch with 8 to10 strong threshing men.

"Uncle Roy showing off his gun collection—seemed like 700 pieces. I liked the pirates' Blunder-bus the best. And I learned the hard way that a boy does not point a gun at any one—not even a toy gun. A valuable lesson.

"July 4th picnics at which Gail would stuff the real cannon at the driveway with powder and newspaper and fire away.

"Sitting on the ice cream freezer, turning the crank until I couldn't turn it any more; then eating fresh peach or strawberry ice cream—wow!

"Swinging on swings under a large limb of a giant Cottonwood tree—seemed like the ropes were 335 feet long. A 9-year-old kid was quite impressed.

"As a 9-year-old, seeing an endless row of batteries and the gasoline engine in the basement so that we could enjoy electric light like city folks—long before the REA arrived.

"The 'travelling grocery store' on a truck that arrived weekly with city-made bread, canned goods—and all that other stuff sold in Danville to the city people.

"Playing, until it was too dark to see, such games as tag, hide and seek, 'Mother, may I,' etc., and playing so hard we couldn't sleep due to leg aches.

"I admired through the years 1932-1992:

"Aunt Della's boundless energy: cooking, milking cows, and later on taking up astronomy and rock collecting.

"Uncle Roy's tremendous mechanical skills.

"Gail, Dolores, and Kevin and Sue increased the farm size several times, and increased corn and bean yields to an unbelievable figure.

"Everyone pitching in all through the 20's, 30's, and 40's to keep the farm going. "Roy, Della, Robert, Roberta, and Gail,

"Thanks for the memories—it was fun!

"Don Colbert, 7/11/92"

Everyone attending was asked to sign the guest book, but some signed individually, some as families, and some not at all. Dolores said she knew quite a few who came, but not all. Dolores and Gail tried to talk to everyone there, many very familiar cousins, but they probably missed some. They all seemed to mix beautifully, and enjoy sharing memories. They were impressed with the posters and notebooks of memories. And there was more than enough food. The pond was active with young swimmers, a line waiting for the swing, and the games had ample players, but sharing memories was the greatest activity.

On Sunday afternoon, an Illinois State Representative presented the Greens with a plaque honoring their 100 years of family ownership, acknowledging Rose Haven Farm as an historic memorial. They were glad the sign on the barn identified it with "Green, 1891." A reporter from *The News Gazette* was there, taking pictures and interviewing some of the guests.

On Sunday evening, the shed was cleared for square dancing, with a caller and an experienced dancer to help the novices.

An arial view of Rose Haven Farm in 2009. Note the highway upper left. Lincoln and Mary would have been amazed at the ease of getting to near-by towns and cities, that took so long by horse and buggy.

Rose Haven Farm

Still Growing and Thriving

Now the old house is gone, but the Rose Haven Farm lives on. Every Green owner added to the farm, now 840 acres. Gail and Dolores bought 40 of those acres near the state road containing the part of Stoney Creek where the Lincoln Green Family picnicked, fished, and learned to swim, and the woods where they hunted wild flowers, and learned to recognize birds and their songs. It's still a great place to wander, finding berries, wildflowers, fishing and hunting. Kevin has planted many, many more trees and cleared the dead wood.

The fourth generation, Kevin Green, grandson of Roy, is farming 1200 acres, Rose Haven Farm's 800 plus 400 rented acres. The 40 acres of woods and stream are cared for, but not farmed. Like his great-grandmother, he has a fascinating background. He was a spelunker—cave explorer, teacher and leader of white-water rafting adventurers, and scuba diving. He added the swimming pool to the farm where he teaches beginning scuba diving, going on to the deep quarry for completing their training. His wife Sue is helping special students in the Oakwood High School. Will his son Travis be the fifth generation to treasure and prosper the Rose Haven Farm? He is, in 2009, working on a master's degree at the University of Illinois, another fifth generation Illini.

Farmers work very hard during the planting and harvesting seasons, but there are times for rest and recreation. Roy thoroughly enjoyed his gun collecting, building the tile shed, and all the tinkering with machinery and old cars. Gail and Dolores enjoyed square dancing and joined groups meeting not only in the Oakwood area, but in surrounding towns. Then they bought an RV and travelled to Florida winters where they found dance groups to join, or went on cruises dedicated to square dancing. Dolores, now a grandmother, is still dancing. Kevin has given up exploring caves, but now finds time to manage white water rafting groups and teach scuba diving, even while farming 1200 acres. Farm life can be very satisfying.

Today, 118 years after Lincoln and Wilbert bought the 240 acres and divided it into two 120-acre farms, Lincoln's 120 has grown to 840 acres. The old barn, now one of several, still proudly displays its origin with the words "Green 1891" legible to all who drive east on U.S. I74, which goes through the edge of the farm. Kevin has added many trees in addition to those Lincoln planted, grown tall and old, around the three homes on the farm: Dolores, Gail's widow lives in the home built soon after they were married, and Lloyd McVey in the one he and Kristina, daughter of Gail and Dolores, built to replace the old Mason house. Sadly, Kristina died in 1993, but Lloyd lives there, keeping the trucks he drives in the oversized garage built for them. Kevin and Sue started their married life in a home converted from one of the shops, but as their family grew, they added rooms and a second story. The swimming pool replacing the old house, is a welcome relief after a hard summer's day work. The pond, still there, enlarged to 60 feet in diameter, now contains many fish, with a big tank also containing fish. The huge equipment needed for so large a farm—plows, planters, corn pickers and reapers, threshers working seven rows at a time—need big sheds and barns. "Gail and Delores built two," Kevin added. Kevin plows, cultivates and gathers his harvest with this huge equipment. He said it takes about an hour to plow one field. The shop also has more and more up-to-date equipment. Gail and Dolores had built two huge cylindrical grain storage bins, with cranes to lift and move the heavy equipment and crops.

The 40 acres containing the woods and section of Stoney Creek that gave so much pleasure to the original Green family were much coveted property. Vivian and Lois Green offered to buy it, but one of the owners refused to sell. Later, Gail and Dolores managed to gain ownership. Kevin has returned the field included in the 40 acres into original prairie, and added many, many trees, clearing out dead trees and underbrush. He is also substituting borders of original prairie for fences in many of his fields. This was in cooperation with a project of the University of Illinois.

The nearby quarry is still used. The deep, deep water is good for scuba training. That quarry was also used way back in the 1930's for swimming for the earlier generations. Kevin is still conducting white-water rafting tours in the mountain streams. And Kevin and Sue, with Dolores, still graciously welcome to the ancestral home of the Green family the progeny of Mary Cranston Green.

All over the United States, the descendants of Lincoln and Mary Esther Green have contributed and are contributing as parents, teachers, businessmen, space scientists, statesmen, writers, artists, even a landscape architect, and yes, farmers—all with integrity and honor. One has even solved a problem eluding particle physicists from Aristotle and Newton to Einstein, by establishing a theory about the origin of particles, and proving it mathematically to within .01% accuracy. In addition to the lovely Rose Haven Farm, Mary Cranston Green has passed on her deep and abiding faith, her formula for successful living, and her wisdom. She has left a wonderful heritage.

Mary Cranston Green with son Roy E. Green, and wife Della Reichard Green.

Mary Cranston Green, from a newspaper article, 1950.

Appendix A

Poems and Essays

—Pre-marraige—1876-1891—

The False Foxglove (1879)

I found you growing in the wood
Beneath the gnarled and aged tress
Where shadows lay.
In grass you stood
And bent toward us in the breeze.
My pulses leaped in glad surprise;
My fingers threaded to clasp your stem.
I bend above love's longing eyes—
I plucked you. Let that one condemn
Who never down your waxen bell
Looked far and deep into your heart
And felt the joy he could not tell
Your form and loveliness impart.

(In Huthman's pasture when I came from school a mile south, because the water was over the foot log.
Before I was married, about 1883 (MCG)

Thanksgiving or Giving Thanks (1884)

About 200 years ago, while this country was yet unexplored by the white man, and the Indians had unmolested possession of forests, on the shores of James River in Virginia was a little band of pilgrims who had crossed the ocean from England to make them a home where they might be free—free in thought and actions. But sickness and famine had discouraged the bravest, and they had determined to abandon their new home, but instead they sought God in prayer, and with renewed hopes and thankful hearts they renewed their task of establishing a land of liberty.

From this event originated our custom of holding, throughout the entire country, one day in each year for a general Thanksgiving to God. It brings to our minds that which is often forgotten, the many blessings we are receiving daily.

All petty things are, or should be, forgotten, that nothing may ruffle the smooth flowing stream of good feeling. Many old New England customs are dying, but this one is spreading as the population of our country increases, and may it continue to spread. We have but to contrast our present condition with that of our forefathers to see wherein we should be thankful. Theirs was the hard lot of pioneers with no protecting government, no free press, no railroads, no steamboats; ours is here in the Nineteenth Century, with the many inventions for our comfort and freedom of thought and action found in no other country. We are, in fact, enjoying the fruit of their labors and in turn, we should do our best to keep the great ball of American Liberty still rolling.

Our personal blessing are many; pause and name them if you can. No man is so badly situated that it might not be worse. Let us then be thankful for all gifts, thankful that Washington was an American, and strive to keep through all the years the hallowed influences of yesterday near us. (Nov. 25, 1884)

Thanksgiving Cheer (1885)

Thanksgiving cheer through all the year
To all who now can willing bow
And say with me, "All thanks to Thee,
Our Guide, our Friend, Who blessings send
For all our needs."
By loving deeds
We hope to pay, if pay we may,
The debt to Thee
Who set us free.
Then give, we pray, each flitting day
A thankful mind to all mankind—
Thanksgiving cheer through all the year.

—M.E. Cranston

Bittersweet (1886)

Foreword to "Bittersweet" Sunday, September 25, 1887

This afternoon I took a walk in the woods—all alone. The forenoon was cold and windy, and I had been feeling sad and discouraged. But the sun shone warm on the southern side of the woods. I gathered some bittersweet and sat down in the sun near a haw tree to pull the leaves from the berries. This is what I thought:

Your leaves are turning to gold, Bittersweet,
And dying with the year.
Soon will the winds blow cold, Bittersweet,
And autumn woods grow sear.
But first in splendor they'll stand, Bittersweet,
In autumn yellow and red,

For they shall be clothed by His hand, Bittersweet,
Whose wonderful works we have read.
The leaves their work will have done, Bittersweet,
Their reward the colors bright.
For mortals at set of their sun, Bittersweet,
With a crown, and garments white.
Last night was a warning, my friend, Bittersweet,
This morning the meadows were hoar.
This warm afternoon will soon end, Bittersweet,
The sunshiny autumn be o'er.
For you must be tried by frost, Bittersweet,
As the heart must be by pain,
Or full fruition is lost, Bittersweet,
Perfection does not attain.
At touch of the Winter King's reed, Bittersweet,
Your orange-red sepals open wide,
Revealing your bright scarlet seed, Bittersweet,
Made perfect, matured, beautified.
While ripened and chastened by God, Bittersweet,
We are purified, strengthened, refined.
For in love, not in anger, His rod, Bittersweet,
Is laid on the heart of mankind.

Athenaeum (1887)

Men of Rome, in by-gone ages,
Poets, lovers, doctors, sages
Came their lamps of wit to lighten
Came their talents more to brighten
Came their sullied names to whiten
To this temple Athenaeum.
Each one sought by deed or story

To achieve some former glory,
Striving ever to excel
Rivals, critics, served them well
As a spur, what 'ere befell,
In their temple Athenaeum.
And perfection glowing ever
Model was to guide endeavor
Model was tho' not attained
Tho' high excellence was gained,
Men of Rome, your hands were chained
In your temple Athenaeum.
Chained as are our hands today
By the finite links of day
Chained by sin to imperfection
To fake paths by indirection
Severed ever from perfection
In your temple Athenaeum.
God the infinite is above
And the perfect His alone
Tho' our souls essay to rise
The wings of faith beyond the skies
They are bound by earthly ties
In our temple Athenaeum.
Nor old oaken wood that burns
And again to dust returns,
Not of crumbling brick or stone
That time worn and ivy grown
Shall at length to earth be thrown
In our temple Athenaeum
Thought ye that narrow walls
Close almost as oxen stalls
The uncovered floor that shadows throw
As hurried footsteps come and go

That the ceiling dark and low
In our temple Athenaeum?
Nay, it is a castle grand
That shall stories of life withstand
A fortress that to you shall be
A stronghold 'til eternity
Gives itself eventually
In our temple Athenaeum.
For beneath, in front, behind
In the emptiness of the mind
Vast expanse of fertile fields
That to labor reaches yield,
Fields of gold tho' half concealed
Round our temple Athenaeum.
Riches, yields of light and beauty
That refined by sense of duty
Will afford rare gems of thought
Pearls of wisdom, truth unsought
In our temple Athenaeum

(Written for the Literature Society in Antioch College)

The Ladder (1887)

Each day is a step on the ladder to time,
And the hours are the links by which we climb.
Whether by studying or tilling the soil,
We are climbing the ladder by honest toil.
While they that study whenever they may
Are getting strength for another day,
And by working with a right good will
Are climbing upward and onward still,
And though they may hope to reach the top,

They'll find the ladder will never stop.
There will always be something more to learn,
Something to study at every turn.
The honest toiling in every clime—
They who improve the fleeting time
Are doers of duty, so are not forgot—
They may climb the ladder tho' humble their lot.
We all are on this ladder of time
And it is for us to say we'll climb.
For they who honestly strive to rise
May find the end far above the skies.

—M.E. Cranston, Antioch College, 1889

Gethsemane (1887)

Gloomy Gethsemane; dark are the shadows
When human friendship and love wholly fail,
When they grow weary and watch not one hour
Or proffer false lips in bitter betrayal.
Bitter Gethsemane, garden of sorrow.
Many the hearts that have struggled therein,
Broken and bruised by somebody's madness,
Crushed by the weight of somebody's sin.
Awful Gethsemane,
There the dear Lord in agony prayed
With heartbreak and soul-break
That the full cup from His lips might be stayed.
Sacred Gethsemane. Take if thou wilt
Thy friends to the gateway, but enter alone
To the infinite God with thy infinite pain
And pray in submission His will to be done.

—Post Marriage—1891-1907—

Merry Christmas

A dear little lane, called Memory,
I follow this time of year,
For it leads me back to other days
And friends that my heart holds dear.
'Tis a happy trail to follow;
Old joys again are new
As I come with a "Merry Christmas"
Down memories to you.

For Ladies Aid

This little garment is sent to you
And this is what we wish you'd do:
The little pocket you plainly see
For a special purpose is meant to be.
Measure your waistline inch by inch.
And see that that measure does not pinch
For each small inch you measure around
Drop into the pocket a penny a pound.
The game is fair, you will admit:
You waist your money, we pocket it.
The money you so freely pay,
Is spent by us in the wisest way.

The Ladies Aid

A tale of helpfulness I'll tell
Extending through the years and start
By saying change of head, 'til well
Can never change the heart—Of Ladies Aid
Our church was ugly, worn and cold
With leaky roof and ceiling low
And windows loose—a creamery of old.
We think and talk and scold—you know—The Ladies Aid
We plan improvements count the cost.
We count our money too—
They don't agree, the cause seems lost,
But happy thought, we tell it to—The Ladies Aid.
We take subscriptions, all we can.
We see our friends in town
And country too and slight no man,
Are not discouraged when they frown—the Ladies Aid.
The fathers sacrifice and toil,
We wear our last year's hat
And wash our dresses when they soil
Or turn them inside out. In that— The Ladies Aid.
And when 'tis finished as you see
With plaster in and outside, too,
The seats are purchased—twenty-three—
In which again 'tis true—The Ladies Aid.
Then carpet old must be replaced—
The trustees shake their head
We shall no longer be disgraced
We'll do it all instead—Of Ladies Aid.
We should have tables, dishes too,
And serve like other folk
And give receptions as they do.

This also shall be done—The ladies Aid.
But time and language fail me now
For casings purchased, coal bills paid,
And things we plan to do and how
Forsooth the money all is made—By Ladies Aid.
I'd tell of aprons and sunhats,
Of quilts and comforters galore,
I'd dwell on jellies, cotton bats the Ladies made
And many labors more—Of Ladies Aid.
But this is what I try to say
To share the burdens with the man
We women sacrifice and pay
Just as they do and we—The Ladies, aid.
And still sometimes there's not enough
To cancel every bill and so
We ask and mean no bluff,
But ask anxiously—when will
The gentlemen give aid.

Spring Beauty

By Lincoln H. Green, for Poetry Club

That met in the Hollow, about 1897—
Mattie and Katie Ilk, Allie Anderson
and I, Mary Cranston Green.
How delicately frail thou are
Of fairy form in every part,
By fairies o'er the hillside spread
And timid, for at Nature's frown
Of clouded sky or hidden sun Thou bendest low thy head.
Yet blessed message dost thou bring
Thou beauty of the early spring,

The gem of hill and mead
Thou speakest of a day to come
When from the cold and silent tomb
A voice shall wake the dead.

Jack in the Pulpit — Indian Turnip

Oh, Jack-in-the-Pulpit, your sister is fair,
The Calla, who lives on the Nile,
But haste not away to dwell with her there
Where tropical aura ever smile.
Your mission is here to preach to our flowers,
Plain dressed in your green and brown suit,
And when they won't hark to the sermons you preach,
Just give them a taste of your root!

The following three poems are from a pressed flower book made for the Botany Club, Christmas 1897.

The Dog-Toothed Violet

As a child I sought most fondly
On the sunny slopes in March
For the red tip of your leaflets
Peeping through the dark, bare earth;
And from that I watched you daily
Growing green and blossoming
Till at length you stood unrivaled:
The first floweret of the spring.

Dutchman's Breeches—Flora's Eardrop

Whether claimed by doughty Dutchman
Or for gentle Flora's ear,
Surely only fairies wear you
In the springtime of the year.
For you are so very dainty
And you play so gay a part,
Did you know you are a cousin
Of the showy bleeding heart?

The Bluebell

Oh Thou, who in olden time
Didst open ears long closed,
Touch these dull ears that we may hear
The Bluebell's fairy chime.

The Answer (1902)

About five years ago this winter
We had a Mothers' Day party here
But what it was we had it for
Is not quite in memory clear.
I think we thought we had done something
To be a little proud of.
I know we praised each other well,
And sang a little louder.
There were speeches, songs and supper;
Singleton and Hanson led.
I know, because I had a paper

And this is what I said:
I fear you have forgotten it.
Also the poem I made
And so to make another one
I read again, "The Ladies Aid"
I hope you see the point I spoke of
As how we women worked and saved
And paid just as the men did,
Then worked still more as Ladies Aid.
We felt we were a step ahead them,
Or they a step behind
And though the load uneven dragged
They didn't seem to mind.
All this is just to let you know that
The Gentlemen have caught up!
And as "Men's Council" for a year now
Almost their end they have brought up.
And now we'll pull together even
All through the Glad New Year.
No load too big, no task too hard,
We'll swing it, never fear.
So here's to our men and women,
Ladies Aid and Council, too,
May they stand for truth and honor
And to church and God be true.

After Lincoln's Death (1907-1914)

Comrades on life's stormy ocean
Mid its struggles and its strife,
Longing in the wild commotion
For a free and noble life,

Keep your eyes upon the hilltops
Bright with many a shining star
They will guide your frail bark safely
"Tho sometimes you sail afar.
Marching, marching ever onward
Still aspiring, still advancing
With a heart that's brave and true
Keep your noble end in view.
Comrades, through this roadway marching,
Weather worn and full of care,
When the desert's heat is parching
Or at rest in valleys fair,
Keep your eyes upon the hilltops
Towering o'er the lowly vale,
'Keep the sun-crowned peak before you,
Never let your courage fail.

A Piece for Ruth (1908)

In Bethlehem's manger long ago,
The little Christ child lay
And not a plan was made to keep
The world's first Christmas Day.
There were no dreams of Santa Claus,
No happy children singing,
No gifts of love from friend to friend,
No sweet-toned church bells ringing.
But angels came to celebrate
His birth with praise and singing,
While wise men, following the star
To Him rich gifts were bringing.
And now we all with happy hearts

Can tell the angel's story,
For with the wise men we have found
Our Christ, the King of Glory.

All Things Now Are Ready (1909)

(Inspired by Booth's Sermon, February14, 1909)

The feast is spread; its reach I see
Through all the ages down to me,
Then onward to eternity.
In present, past, and bye-and-bye,
All one; but our flesh-holden eye,
Forsooth, can neither end descry
The table? 'Tis God's gracious plan
To feed the hungry soul of man
That lives and labors here a span.
The dishes surely you can see
The flower-cups and leaf of tree,
The floating cloud and laughing sea,
The nests of birds and singing brooks,
The Inspired Word and other books,
The warm handclasps and friendly looks
Filled to the overflowing brim,
Or heaped above the highest rim
With nourishment supplied by Him?
And though with springing step or slow
The generations come and go,
The food remains, and this I know:
The Bread of Life cannot grow stale,
The Living Waters ne'er shall fail,
The healing leaves shall e'er prevail.
And, oh, the wondrous company:

The good, the great, the spirit free
Of every age partake with me.
'Tis God, Himself, the host, doth call,
"Ho, every one, come one, come all
And hunger no more, nor thirst."

Made Free Through Mountains

Come to the mountaintop, Christ, and rested be;
Behold the kingdoms of the world from sea to sea.
Mark well their glory; see the fame of men who lead
Their hosts in battle or in their courts with power plead.
Thrill to the praise of greatness in whatever field
And hear the luring whisper, "If you will but yield
First place within your heart, forsake the One Divine
For me, a place among the greatest shall be thine."
Listen, yet to your inner self, and to Him be true
And another height, another glory shines for you,
A glory as the sun to pale moonlight.
For there transfigured, with His raiment shining white,
Your Lord, to wondering eyes a glimpse of heaven shall give,
And bid you in the hope of immortality to live.
Stand thus the test, obey the heavenly vision too,
Or learn another vision waits for you—
Mt. Calvary, the place of sacrifice. Consent
To pain and darkness, death, then shall the veil be rent
That kept you from the holiest place, and you shall be
Raised to abundant life and by the Son made free.

—Mary Cranston Green, (Singleton Theme)

Mark 14: 14-15

There is a room within my heart
Where many friends have tarried for a while
And passing, left behind a fragrant memory,
A dear companionship and happy smile.
An upper room and large, love furnished for my guests,
And I have it ready, Lord, for Thee.
Wilt come, most honored one, most loved,
And eat the sacred Passover with me?
For I remember many dangers passed
And realize that Thou wert leading me
By light at night, by shadow through the day,
And I recall the pathway through the sea,
The song of triumph and the hunger satisfied,
Thy patience in the wilderness of doubt
When fear possessed me, and I murmured sore
And how with loving care you led me out.
Until in Thee I glimpse the promised land
And I again would thank Thee—
Come, wilt thou?
And henceforth, when I eat the bread and drink
Life's wine, I'll feel
Thy presence near as I do now.

Consecration

I bring my Alabaster box,
Dear Lord, and break it at Thy feet.
Oh, may it be a good to Thee
As costly incense sweet.
For in it I have kept with care

The precious things that all the years
Of life have brought to me—
The mingled hopes and fears.
My childish fancies of Thyself,
Youth's longing to attain,
The wiser dream of womanhood,
Ambitions that remain,
The happiness from field and sky,
The gladness of the spring,
The uplift from all outdoor things
The passing seasons bring.
The bitterness of trust betrayed,
The grace that overcame,
The sympathy and joy and help
Of friends in more than name,
The fragrance of a love that was,
Dried rose leaves of the past,
The grief that brought Thee near to me,
The shadows round me cast,
The sacred thoughts of motherhood,
The care, the strength, it brought,
The finite blent with infinite,
The wisdom dearly bought.
The present duties to be done,
Occasions to be seized,
The busy days for hands and brain,
The hunger unappeased,
The burden of the coming years, The hope of joys to be,
These are the measure of my life—I bring them all to Thee.

—Mary Cranston Green, Jan.14, 1909, Urbana

The First Psalm

(Prayer Meeting, assigned by Mr. Wilhelm, 1909)

I like the beautiful simile that David gives of a man,
The picture he shows to me I'll draw for you if I can.
There first in Jordan's grassy plain,
Stretching from bluff to river brink,
Gray-brown awaiting the later rain, the creeks are all dry, I think.
The trees on the slope are crooked and small;
Their thirsty leaves droop down,
But close to the river, magnificent still,
Stands a beautiful tree, alone.
Its branches strong to the breezes
Spread make a shade for passers-by,
While the rich, dark green of its leaves overhead
Delight the weary eye.
In burning heat, unwithered, it stands,
Its fruits unfailing grow,
For its roots reach down through the barren sands
To the living waters below.

—Mary Cranston Green

A Christmas Meditation

It needs must be that Christ should give
His life that sinful man might live,
But why not come, as in olden day
The angels came—as He went away—
A man full grown? Why exiled be
So long before His ministry?
Was the cross not enough?
Could it be, as I have sometimes thought,

He came as He did and humbly wrought
At a trade, all those commonplace years,
That he might know the hopes and fears
Of a commonplace life? For we
Give most freely our sympathy
To experiences we have known—
Where the burdens arc like our own.
But, did He need to learn?
Tonight my heart burns as I ponder long
That not unto death does life belong.
He gave His life most when He lived it here
That mortals might know how very near
The divine may be each step of the way.
For angels are nearer each mother today,
And children in loving favor grow
Because of that childhood long ago.
And manhood has gained a purer tone
Through study of His as the years have flown;
And friends are dearer, it seems to me,
Because of that friendship in Bethany.
So toiler and tempted and troubled may know
The Father is near. Christ proved it so.
And do you not feel, in wonderful love
By the gift of His Spirit from above,
He gives His life still?

My Easter 1910

I knelt one day in my garden path
Beside a desolate bed,
Where plants once bent with fragrant bloom
Stood straight and bare, some dead.

The birds were flitting from shrub to shrub
The sun lay warm on the ground,
And I was not sad with thought of the past
'Tho none of its beauty I found;
For under the leaves I knew that the bulbs
Were lifting their blossoms fair,
And the rich dark earth had softened been
For new hopes to be planted there.
Today I knelt in that path again
To gather my daffodils
With their silver stars and golden cups;
Their fragrance the garden fills.
And I know that after the winters of life
God gives us beautiful springs
If we yield our bared hearts to the warmth of His love
And nurture the seed that He brings.

—1911 - 1923—

The Botany Bulletin for October 1911

The bulletin's come, with pleasure I read
All that's written therein, yes, yes indeed. Mr. Herr,
I'll divide, and promise you now
If not oil for your lamp, some hay for your cow.
Miss Laughlin, you'd not have asked us in vain
To share in your walk nor in even the rain'
My friends are the same, though we always ride
To the scene of the search—there's the steep hillside!
And you shall have "Stips," if that is the name.
Miss Clark and Mrs. Claflin, our number's the same.

Again, Mr. Webb has nothing to say,
We'll forgive him, and hope that next time he may.
That you're not overworked, Mr. Rood, do not boast
For I've done as you said, collected, and most
Of the plants are yet to be named. Oh, well,
More time is coming with winter perhaps.
I'll tell Of my summer. Shall I prattle of household care
That left in each week scarce an hour to spare?
Of chickens and children, of garden and cow,
Of sewing and mowing and full hands now:
Shall I tell of the trips I wanted to take
To woodland and stream, when I felt in me wake
The longing for wild things when I knew the green ferns
Unwound their long fronds where the dark river turns
At the foot of the hill, or dreamed on its crest
New flower were blooming, awaiting my quest?
Oh no, not of these, for I know each of you
Has a daily round of duty, too;
And I fear that by all some pleasures were missed,
That in vacation plans, were down on the list.
Why mention the things that occasion regret
When the happiest way is just to forget
We have disappointments while we gladly recall
The pleasures that also come to us all?
I'll tell of the grass diet once Miss Laughlin scorned,
Still teaching the truth Nebuchadnezzar learned,
And the rare thing, as Mr. Herr said before,
That we think far afield may be found at our door,
For, craving new forms of beauty and charm,
To add to my knowledge, I went out to the farm;
Spring flowers were gone, "was so late in the year,
And the really wild places are not very near.
The nearest, in fact, is two miles away

And in searching its secrets I spent but one day;
Of that, more anon; you'll admit as I pass,
There wasn't much left but to study the grass.
And that was enough. Delight grew apace.
Mr. Rood said it would, as I studied the grass
Of its delicate forms, I have seen all my life!
And who would have guessed that highway and field
And orchard and garden, such treasures could yield?
For from tough little Jensen to waving swamp-grass
About fifty specimens I've gathered, en mass.
For grasses alone not a trip did we make
Yet on business or pleasure not a ride we take,
Not even from church, without scanning the way
With expectant delight, as son said, for "more hay,"
'Twas almost like going to some country new,
So much was disclosed.
The children searched, too.
In the garden the crowless arrow feet were a sight;
When we pulled the foxtails we suffered no bite.
Now were we amazed by the soft
Ticklegrass Growing there with the others, too abundant, alas!
While pulling them up sweet revenge I took—
I called them the names that I found in the book!
Fragrostis, Megastachny and Pos,
Sataris Glanca, but I'll inflict with no mo'e
Of these jaw-breaking names;
At least not until I know them myself. Then I will,
Having mounted and labeled all that I pressed,
Perhaps be enabled to mention the rest.
Now pardon the flaws in this rhythm, I pray,
I hope they don't mar what I wanted to say:
There are kinks in my yarn, or breaks in the thread
Of my discourse, by some interruptions.

As I said At the first, I am busy, and from time to time
As I followed the work, I have added a rhyme.

Judas (November, 1914)

You walked in fellowship and converse sweet
Among the sunny fields of Judah's plain
With One who from the lily and the grain,
Every well and wayside and from rippened wheat
Cold gain for every life some lesson meet.
You heard no needy call to him in vain
And see him have the mastery of pain.
Three wondrous years you followed holy feet
And yet, oh Judas, with the traitorous lips
From such high place you fell to this
And made your name a synonym of shame
Like one, who reaching perfect heights, yet slips
Into the chasm, so with empty kiss,
Love's symbol masking faithless heart, you came.

(Prayer meeting at Worley's, Nov. 5, 1914)

As Jacob

When first we feel His presence near
We cry, "How dreadful, God is here."
And cower, full of fear.
For we behold the cost of sin,
We plead, "Oh, Savior, take me in,
Let me Thy heaven win."
"Forgive, protect and grant us peace,
Prosperity and faith increase,
Bid fear and troubling cease.

And Thou henceforth our God shall be
One tenth Thou givest return to Thee."
Raise Bethel selfishly.
But when we meet God face to face,
Behold his majesty and grace,
And see His holy place
In us is born a new ideal
Of life and service and we feel
Unselfish loves appeal.
Old passions, old desires cry
For old dominion—will not fly
So wrestling still must die.
The shrunken sinews of our pride
Relax; then peace and trust abide,
Our all is satisfied.
And so, victorious in this trial
Of self o'er self and its denial,
We name Penial.

(Prayer meeting at Worley's Nov. 5, 1914)

The Old Schoolhouse

Oh, little we see when looking without
Of the merit that lies within
The rich, the witty that lies within
Not all the praises win,
For we who do the best we can
On each of life's school days
Are counted as worthy in God's sight
As they who win men's praise.
The old school house was but a case
That sheltered jewels rare.
We know not what the influence

Of children gathered there.
'Twill be, when as men and women
They scatter the jewels away
The gems of thought and learning
May move the world some day.
The old school house has fallen now
Sold for small, nay a paltry sum.
A new one stands in its place today
And hither to learn we come.
But we hope to do as well
In our studies from day to day
In the years that are coming, as we did
In the years that have passed away.

—1924-1928—

Babies

(by Richard Green, when helping develop and print pictures of babies)

Just look at the babies we have here!
Each one is his fond parents' pride,
I am sure it is the finest collection
You ever could find if you tried.
There are babies and babies and babies!
They come from all parts of the town.
They have curly hair, straight hair and no hair,
They have black eyes, blue eyes and brown.
They have lungs as their neighbors could tell you,
But words they have only a few
And we hope that they'll never learn many
Except they are good words and true.

They have bodies to tenderly care for;
They have minds to be lovingly taught;
They have souls to be won for the Savior.
God help us to teach as we ought!
Oh, bless them, dear Father in heaven,
This prayer would we offer to Thee,
And when they are babies no longer,
Then "children in Christ" may they be.

That Baby

(by Martin Green, printing pictures)

One little row of ten little toes,
To go along with a brand new nose/
Eight little fingers and two little thumbs
That are just as good as sugar plums—
That's baby.
One little pair of new round eyes
Like a little owl's, so big and wise.
One little place they call a mouth
Without a tooth from north to south.
That's baby.
Two little cheeks to kiss all day
Two little hands, so in the way,
A brand new head, not very big
That seems to need a brand new wig—
That's baby.
Dear little row of ten toes!
How much we love them, nobody knows.
Ten little kisses on mouth and chin—
What a shame he isn't a twin!
That's baby.

His Kingdom Come

A "man of sorrows" and acquainted with grief
Alone he bore the pain of His Gethsemane
That we might understand and bring relief
When in the garden dark fainting with doubt are we.
"No man His generation shall declare,"
And yet, when Jesus drew the children close
I'm sure he felt the same protecting care
And tender love that fills a Father's heart.
He must have yearned to keep them pure and sweet,
His Kingdom's own, so smiling, blessed them there.
The rich are they who seek
God's kingdom first, then share
Their blessings with the meek,
Poor children of His care.

—Undated Poems—

"If"

"If I were you," You say to me "I clearly see
What I would do"
But yet, If you were I, It seems to me
As dull you'd be As now seem I
And so If I were you I'd not be bold
In how I told What I would do.
You see If you were I And I were you
In what we'd do No change I spy
So now Since you are you
And I am I Each can but try Her own to do.

Give Smiles

One smile is worth a thousand frowns
To cheer our friends, I'm sure,
And oft for little ills of life
It is a magic cure.
Yes, self-constraint is a glorious thing,
Without it religion is vain.
To bridle our tongues and tempers, too
Is a power we strive to attain.
But what is revealed in the moments of life,
Oh, my friend, when the self is off guard?
When from the full heart the mouth speaketh out?
We need then the control of our God.

Life Journey

The morning star is twinkling
Just at the peep of day
And we in our beds lie dreaming
Of the future far away/
The glorious time that's coming
And the laurels we shall win
We see not the trials awaiting
With the feet inured to sin.
But now the sun is shining
Hides the stars with blankets blue
It calls us back to the present
With the alarms "Up and Do."
Lie not there idly dreaming.
Those who win must work.
Then up while the morning's purest,

Strive not your task to shirk.
Put your foot upon the ladder
With the words "I climb."
Set your goal upon the summit;
Improve the fleeting time.
Rely on your own resources.
Look not to man for aid,
For God alone can guide you
Through the trials He has made.
Each effort makes you stronger
Further up the hill,
Then on and do not falter.
You can triumph still.
'Tis morn. We are no longer dreaming.
Our race is half way run.
But we hear the mornings warning!
Have we yet our race begun?
Have we reached the very summit
Of the mighty hill of life?
Or are we standing idle'
Afraid of toil and strife?
Trust in God and fear not
But work with a resolute will.
Obey the commands given
And we may triumph still.
Some have reached the shining summit.
Some have not begun to climb.
"We were waiting," say they sadly,
"For some better, easier climb
When the pathway seemed less troubled
But alas too late we know
That the pathway never opens
But to those who toil below."

And to those who now are drifting
Let us send a word of warning:
If you really wish to triumph
You can start best in the morning.

The Pessimist
(by the editor of the *Urbana Courier*)

Whoever saw a farmer smile
Or speak in happy vein
When of them stops to talk awhile?
It's always too much rain
Or else it's too dad blasted dry,
Or frosts will kill the crop,
And he's chock full of reasons why
The market's bound to drop.
A chronic mourner is this bird.
Who tills the verdant soil.
His woes the year around are heard
For naught has been by Hoyle.
As pessimist he takes the cake
He thrives on sighs and moans;
For him life's one long bellyache,
His system racked with groans.

The Answer: It Seems Some of 'em Smile

"Whoever saw a farmer smile?"
I often have, my son,
For I have lived for quite a while
Where farming's being done.
He smiles when discontented strike

At city rents and bills,
And thanks the Lord for lot unlike
While His green earth he tills.
He smiles when needed rains come down,
When hungry mouths are fed.
He smiles at corn silk turning grown,
At apples hanging red.
He smiles at gains that work no harm.
Enough! But mark it down,
The smiling farmer's on the farm,
Not loafing 'round in town.
Yours truly, Mary

Witty Sayings for Newspaper Columns

You and me are not like folk,For I'll be stillest when I croak.
Unlike his owner, what a joke,

My colt is worth more when he's broke.
—(Silly wit for the *Commercial News*, 1925)

The fowl, unlike us, is dead
If he but once does "lose his head." (May 1900)

When I the best-lines nest produce, I am the most unlike the goose.
I'm sending reason, four at least, Why I'm not like a barnyard beast.

Memories of Deceased Lincoln H. Green

Another brave soldier has fallen
That had enlisted in Christ's battlefield.
He felt it was His voice calling.
And he thought it his duty to yield.
For years he had lived in the service
And fought as only a true soldier can,
And no matter what it cost him,
He went at the Lord's command.
As a Father he was so devoted,
As a husband so faithful and true,
And to the poor or the needy
He did what his hands found to do.
Of a true manly example
None could more fully compare
And we feel that wherever he went
He left a good influence there.
And we're sure his life was worth living,
If reflected on our lives and let shine
Would light up our pathway to heaven
Where we'll know not the sorrow or time.
And the flowers as a last tribute was given him
Were of greatest respect and love,
But the flowers had strewn in the pastures while here
Can only be reckoned above.

Appendix B

The Pond

by Mary Cranston Green

In reading the various papers as I have for years, I am strongly impressed not only by the continued improvement in make-up and illustrations and by the irresistible spirit of progress as shown in the articles on better fields, better farming, better stock, better dogs, better machinery, better buildings, but also by the almost utter lack of display for the better growth and all around development of the boys and girls. They have their nice rooms in the new homes where they sleep and spend a few hours in bad weather, if there is nothing else to do. Oh yes, they have the advantage of all the improvements about the home and farm the same as the elder people. Yes, yes. They have books and music and schools, of course. All these carefully supervised by elder ones. I mean something *besides* these, something that will give them opportunity for the free growth of originality and individuality that comes best in delightful play, unconscious of supervision.

Just such an opportunity has developed at our farm home in the shape of a small pond. I freely admit that no such thing was thought of when the pond was made.

Our farm is as level and black as any that can be found on the prairies of Illinois, but there is a slight slope in one corner near the roadway in which grows a big cottonwood tree (the only native tree on the place), twenty rods from the house. In this corner, twenty years ago, stood my husband's home and mill for making sorghum, which he did on a large scale. To elevate the mill so that the juice could run directly to the pans (vats), two men with scrapers and teams spent a week scraping the dirt from the corner into a small hill. Later, in a few years, the sorghum lot became a garden, and the hollow a pond, "The Pond," the delight of the children. In it were put the small fish saved on fishing trips and from ditches. A few dry seasons these fish were kept in a large stock tank for a few weeks, until the rains.

The two men spent another week enlarging and deepening the pond so that it went dry less frequently. We planted water lilies, cat tails, water plantain, and arrow head in one edge, and a grove of different kinds of native trees in the west. We soon dug up the cat tails, however, for they spread too fast and did not die down out of the way of the ice, as the other plants did.

The fish became large enough to help keep down the mosquitoes and the scum, and in the pond all the children learned to swim—Even Roberta, the granddaughter. They learned to paddle a raft, and sorghum-pan boat. It has been their undisputed realm with only occasional suggestions from their elders. They built a dressing room on the bank, and high and low diving boards. In low water, they dug caves in the bank and walls in the bottom, connecting the walls by canals, and dipping the water playing at irrigation.

They lay on the grassy banks, or on the sand scraped from the bottom, or sat on the boulders brought in from the fields and mused and watched the waxy birds come for a drink and a bath. They watched the many bugs and dragon flies, but most of all they watched the tiny fish and the ever-interesting change of the tadpole into a frog; then caught the frog for his delicious hind legs. They have learned much natural history in a way never to be forgotten. And I knew where they were.

Two weeks ago, the oldest son Roy, now head farmer here, spent another week with the team until it is now about 60 feet across and eleven feet deep, which is also down to living water. Later we employed a drag line. Part of the sand and clay was spread out to the north for a tennis court. Most of it was used to make a coasting grade from the small hill among the trees to the surface of the ice, for the pond became an ice rink in the winter. The tennis court became a flower garden in 1939, and remained a garden of natural wild and perennial flowers until the Freeway, Route Number 74 took a part of the area.

The beautiful fragrant water lilies, double white, added to the charm of the place, until the pond became a duck pond. Boxes of the lily blooms were sent to the girls when away in school, and to friends, and received by all with delight.

We now live in Urbana for the school term, to avail the children of the High School and the University of Illinois, but spend the summer on the farm. This summer the fifteen-year-old boy—Vivian—stretched a cable from high in the cottonwood tree, a mammoth tree by now, far across the pond, attaching a swing to a strong pulley wheel, and down this had many a joy ride, often dropping down into the water.

Since beginning this article, I have asked the children—five of the seven still live at home—one by one as they come in, "What part of the farm home do you think of with the most pleasure:" Big and little, boys and girls, answered without hesitation, "The Pond!" There is no fear the boys will not go back to the farm, for they can hardly wait for summer to do so.

For three weeks or more of labor, what else could you crowd into so much pleasure, or for that matter, into a hundred feet square of almost waste land? Also, the pond serves a purpose not mentioned in the pleasures above—in times of heavy rain, it serves as a run-off for flood waters.

I think such a pond could be made on almost every farm, set down to living water, or at least deep enough to go dry only in the driest seasons. Let those who would not spend even so much time for pleasure and growth alone remember, remember the fish; remember the ice for the family ice house.

(The foregoing was estimated to have been written originally in about 1915, with more recent information added:)

Postscripts by Della Reichard Green: "I recall that when a sizable pond in Oakwood was going dry, that we put their fish in this pond, and then let the windmill run for three weeks to supply needed water to this pond. We benefitted our well by getting all the silt out of it, and ended up with better water.

"I raised lots of white Peking ducks and had sufficient feathers each picking time to make a good pillow. The turtles had to be controlled. They would grab a baby duckling by the legs and pull it under to its death. The men shot the turtles on sight. Really, the turtle eggs were quite an item, too.

"Attempts at raising water lilies and ducks together were in vain, and a source of regret in the last 50 years. Since 1939 when Mother Green came again to the farm to live, the remaining years until 1964, when she entered a nursing home until her death in 1965, she had a good flower garden only."

Postscript by Katherine R. Inman 2009: "The Pond is still used, now only for raising fish, for there is also a large swimming pool on the farm. I, too, remember the fun all of us cousins had in that pond in the 1920's and 30's."

Appendix C — History of Oakwood

HISTORY OF OAKWOOD 1870-1930

Class III, Intermediary, of the Methodist Sunday School Historian:

Mary Cranston Green

TO THE FRIENDS OF OAKWOOD

In presenting this brief history of Oakwood, with the desire of stimulating a greater interest and appreciation of our spot of the great earth, Class Three of the Intermediate Department of the Methodist Sunday School wishes to acknowledge its indebtedness for the information herein to the many loyal, longtime residents of this place and the Lottie E. Jones *History of Vermilion County, 1911*, and the H.W. Beckwith History of the same, 1879.

Vermilion County, organized in 1826, of which Oakwood Township is a part, was first explored and made known to the world by the French, exploring the Wabash River and its tributaries. The earliest known proprietors were the Piankeshaw Indian tribe, belonging to the Miami Confederacy. The last tribe, the Pottowatomies, were dispossessed and moved west in 1818. While moving they camped for some time on the Dave Fowler farm.

There are supposed to be Indian relics and a burial ground in the woods on the east side of Stony Creek about three-fourths of a mile south of the Oakwood Township High School. Several years ago two strangers went to this spot, held a short ceremony, and broke a bottle of wine, saying nothing to anyone. It was guessed they were descendants of some Indian buried there.

There is an Indian burial ground near Kessler hill, on the east side of the Middle Fork, where the bluff is nearly one hundred feet high. It is a plateau of several acres, and commands a fine view of both streams. Here in 1852 was found a silver peace medal presented to the Indians by General Putnam after the treaty of Vincennes in 1792. It represents George Washington receiving the peace-pipe from and Indian brave who has thrown his tomahawk at the foot of a tree. At the same time was found a British medal made in 1786. Both medals, with parts of a skeleton, were supposed to have been washed from the grave of Kesis, the great Chief (see Beckwith History). There was a large Kickapoo Indian village at the mouth of the South Fork, probably destroyed by General Hopkins in the war of 1812.

The first white man to learn, early in 1800, of the salt springs in use by the Indians on the bluff of Salt Fork about one-half mile west of the Middle Fork, was Joseph Barron, soldier and interpreter for General Harrison. Because of the hostility of the Indians, no attempt was made to work these springs until after the treaty in 1819. Barron and a party rediscovered them on September 22, 1819. In December, Seymour Treat brought his family to the springs and built a cabin 14-feet-square of small round logs. It was the first white settlement or house in Vermillion County. In 1821 or 1822 a Mr. Bailey built on Stony Creek. He soon sold to Harvey Luddington and the creek was known as Luddington's Branch.

In a short time, Mr. Walker built a little farther on the stream near the present site of Muncie in a point of timber which was called Walker's Point. Soon many settlements or houses were built along the Salt Fork. Major Vance, who began operating the salt works in 1824, built his house where Missionfield now is. Moses Izzard and Mr. Barkly built near the Kickapoo burial ground. Wm. Cox and Gen. Cadle James Norris and

Henry Oakwood are others among the first settlers. Conkeytown was begun in 1861, Newton in 1837 or 1838.

By the time Oakwood Township was formed in 1868 all the land was occupied by pioneers, many of whose descendants still live in Oakwood vicinity. Oakwood Township, twelve miles east and west, and six miles north and south, was set off from Pilot Vance and Catlin Township through the efforts of George A. Fox, then supervisor of Vance Township.

The laying of the Indiana, Bloomington and Western, later called the Big Four Railroad, across the Township in 1869 was a big event in the lives of these first settlers. Until this time they got their mail and most of their supplies from Danville, nine miles away across the unbridged Middleboro. The roads were often impassable. There were Post Offices in Pilot near Newtown and at Conkeytown where mail was brought weekly on horseback.

A railroad is of little value without a station, so the question of where to locate was paramount. The present site seemed best for east was rough timber land, west was low and swampy ground, and south a half-mile on the Old State Road at Blue Corner was a small store, a school house, a Methodist Church called Finley Chapel, and a blacksmith shop. The land was owned by William Harrison, who gave 10 acres for the site. Others gave money and the right-of-way across their farms.

It is difficult to determine why the name Oakwood was chosen. Perhaps it was because Oakwood Township was already named. Perhaps because Illinois has a Harrison and a Harrisonville. Perhaps because Henry Jefferson Oakwood rode many miles on horseback interviewing and persuading the officials to locate the station here. At any rate, Oakwood Station it became, and the plat for the town surveyed April 14, 1870.

Early in the spring of 1870, the depot was built. An amusing and gratifying incident was the mistake of unloading the depot material here that was intended for Danville. The mistake was not discovered until the building was begun, making it too late to change, so Oakwood was proud of a better station than Muncie whose plat was recorded in 1875, or Fithian, plat filed April 8, 1879. Mr., Frank Davis remembers driving the first wagon across the rails on Oakwood Street.

There was but one house, really a cabin, its siding up and down, stood where John Davidson's house now stands on South Street by a big cottonwood tree. Soon after the depot was built, Lon Campbell, a farmer, built two houses to rent or sell. One burned in 1874 and the other is now the home of James Wilson, the second house east of the Methodist church, on West Collert Street. It was at one time a hotel.

The first warehouse where grain was bought stood near where the lime house is, and was also built by Lon Campbell. It was run by Louis Verey, Campbell's son-in-law, who also taught country school, and was also Sunday School Superintendent later. He lived in the warehouse. The third house was built where the bank now stands on the Northwest corner of Scott and Finley. Bill Harper once lived there, also Mr. Southard. The house was moved east on Finley and is now the home of Henry Jackson.

The first store stood on the south side of East Main, and was run by Johns and Milton Stewart of Danville. It burned in 1871. Henry Dulin built the second store and Brown built where the interurban station is now. J.A. Saylor, Wm. Stillwell, Mr. Applegate, Joe Truax, and John Young are some of the other early store keepers.

The first drug store, located on the south side of East Main was owned and operated by Henry Dulin, Dr. Dulin's brother. He was also the postmaster. He was bought out in 1882 by his uncle, J.A. Saylor, who built the seventh dwelling on the lot where Z.S. Saylor now lives on East Finley Avenue. He built the brick store on East Main in 1881, the first brick building in town.

James Conley was the first section foreman, and Dick Dirley was the first telegraph operator.

Dr. Hewitt and Mrs. Dr. Guinan seem to have practiced medicine in the country around about before the Station was built, but Dr. Gavin was the first in town. Dr. Dulin came while Dr. Gavin was here. Then came Doctors Carter, Leeks, Boggess, Hensley Collins, Fox, Lottman, Winslow, Williams, Chaffee and Snyder. Dr. W.T. Snyder graduated in Louisville, Kentucky and has been here nineteen years since 1911. There was bad smallpox epidemic in 1871.

Oakwood never had a saloon, but Bill Hall, nephew of Wolfington, began selling beer by the gallon in a small place near the warehouse. When warned by John Saylor that he was about to be raided, he reluctantly consented to quit.

There were thirteen homes in Oakwood Station when the Longstreth family moved into town in 1876.

Wm. Handail was the blacksmith at Blue corner. Jacob James was the first in Oakwood. His shop was under the big cottonwood. The following have since been blacksmiths here: Ihue Shoot, Ed Lawler, Billy Neal, Chas. Peterson, now on the State Road, and Brad Neal, the last named still here, and has been since 1893. The first hardware store was built in 1892 by John Saylow, but burned September 24, 1897, in a fire which burned several stores and the warehouse. After this fire some of the stores were rebuilt on South Scott Street.

The first lumber yard was run by F.L. Hill, who sold to Trent Brothers and Elliott. They were operating in 1907. J.S. Mason entered the firm in 1913, and it became Mason and Trent. The present complete line of hardware was added after the Oddfellow block was built in 1892-23. They occupy the east side of the first door.

The Oakwood Cemetery, on the State Road, was set apart in 1892. Mrs. Minnie Meade was the first interred there. Soon many brought the bodies of relatives from other cemeteries. James Knee in December 1892, and E.P. Sampson in Jan. 1893 were buried there, Rev. Creighton of the Christian Church preaching both funeral sermons.

The first barber shop was in 1887. E.N. Longstreth traded rare bushels of corn and one dozen hens for a barber chair which he loaned to John Cole, colored, the first barber. Cole was not a success, so Mr. Longstreth selected a comb; clippers, and a pair of scissors, and took over the shop. For a time he cut hair for nothing, for anyone who would let him for practice. The first time he used the clippers, he got them caught in the hair, and they had to be taken apart to remove them. Frank Crawford was the "patient." In 1891, in addition to the barber shop, Mr. Longstreth was mending shoes, selling sandwiches, and soft drinks. He began helping his father mend shoes when twelve years old. They then used wooden pegs, often split from thin sections of maple limbs. He has been in various businesses through the years—liveryman, photographer, and harness maker. When his son Oral came back from the Great War, they started the present restaurant, April 18, 1920. The popular "Blue Room" was added in 1924.

Burke and Collings, in 1890 were the first undertakers. They had no hearse. John Redman was the first to have a hearses about 1894. After Mr. Redman's death, his son Vernier conducted the business until he died in 1929. J.H. Cawthon. His assistant has been the undertaker since. He is also postmaster.

The present elevator was built after the fire in 1897 by B.B. Minor. It is now owned and operated by Russell Rodgers and Chas. Hillman. They also have the Bronson Brothers, and Muncie elevators.

W.D. Roberts built a frame building for a general store on South Scott Street in 1907, and has been in business near the same place ever since except two years he spent in Texas. The back building was created about 1915. Van Trimble has conducted the Company Store, on East Main Street for fifteen years, seven years for Hartshorne

Brothers Coal Company was there for eight years for the Electric Mine Company. Their store has recently been consolidated with the Company Store in Danville. Mr. Trimble retains his position.

A.T. Snyder, owner of the lower part of the Woodman Building on East Main Street has had his store there for eight years. He came from Iowa where he had had a store for fourteen years. J.S. Miller has been Interurban Station agent for nine years. Lloyd Nichols has been section foreman about two years for the I.T.S. Harry Killion, proprietor of the Killion Novelty Shop in Old Saylor brick store building, opened this year and has many interesting things. Wm. Fagaly, proprietor of the general store on the west side of Main Street and Scott Street, was the first to occupy the new store room. He has been there seven years. He previously had a store at Flat Rock for five years. A.J. Fern, agent and telegraph operator for the Big Four has been located here sine Jan. 1, 1918, thirteen years. John Prichard has been section foreman since 1917. Mr. St. John has been the barber for about two years.

There have been garages and filling stations in Oakwood since the wide state pavement was laid on the old State Road south of the town. They have gone to old Blue Corner. Sailor's service station and the Texaco station were built there in 1925. The R.&S. (Richter & Saults) garage on the State Road is operated by Gordon Bridgeman.

The First State Bank of Oakwood was opened in 1907 on the northeast corner of Scott Street and Finely Avenue in the brick building where the telephone office now is. Directors were Mr. Van Allen, Mr. Johnson and Mr. Seymour & Co. The present building northwest corner of Scott and Finley was erected in 1918. Charles Andrews has been the cashier since its beginning. Lucille Wooden, bookkeeper, has been in the bank nearly seven years.

Oakwood had a newspaper for about five years—*The Oakwood News*. It was first edited and published by W.D. Rodgers in 1909. It started as a four page paper, but became an eight page. Subscription price was one dollar per year. Mr. Rodgers edited it about three years, a Mr. Rose about six months, then the Commercial Club of Oakwood took it over. Mr. Booe was publisher. It was discontinued for it was not a financial success, but was much enjoyed by the citizens, several of whom were contributors.

There was an interesting item of a robbery in Muncie in the fall of 1903. It was telephoned from there that the robbers were coming this way on a hand car. A railroad tie was laid across the track. When the hand car struck it the three colored robbers were thrown off and ran for the Hillman cornfield. A few shots were fired, but most agreed that most of the citizens ran the other way. The following poem by Z.A. Saylor, celebrating the event, was published in the *Oakwood News*:

The Charge of the Village Dads

by Dell Saylor

The phone bell rang quite loudly.
It was twelve o'clock, midnight,
As "central" took the message,

his face grew deathly white!
The news conveyed was tragic—
"Three 'coons' from Muncie fled.
Were headed east on hand car—
Capture alive or dead."
The Village Dads were summoned.
"Arm, arm" was then the cry.
The Dads responding to the call
prepared to do or die.
The rattle of the hand car soon broke
the silence still,
On, on it came with fearful speed,
unchecked by curve or hill.
The Dads, brave men of fertile brain,
quickly a scheme was planned.
They pile obstruction on the track,
and this then strongly manned.
The hand car now hove into sight.
It soon must hit the "grit"
Then great would be the capture,
and the Dads would sure be "it."
Behind the barricade they crouched,
waiting with baited breath,
Not knowing what fate had in store.
To some it might mean death.
The fateful moment came at last.
"Ca-biff," Oh what a spill!
Bang bang, the guns began to bark!
How many did they kill?
The shots kept popping everywhere,
just like a real old battle.
Like old Bull Run, or Gettysburg
with shot and shell and rattle.

When firing ceased, the roll was called:
Not one had "hit the dust"!
Ham Rush received a slight flesh wound,
but he just "stewed and cussed."
As for the coons, did they escape?
To say the least, they're cunning,
And from the latest we have heard,
these coons are still a-running.

As early as 1893, John Young, the store keeper, had a public telephone, the only one, but a Ridgefarm Co. put in an exchange office. Then they used poles, rails, and boards, and later smooth wire about 1881.

When Henry Jefferson Oakwood bought the eighty north of his fathers where his son Charles now lives, the neighbors were sorry that a young man should invest in such "worthless property," it was so wet. He proved his faith. His first underground drainage was of two hickory logs hewn flat on one side, laid as a Vee, then covered by a hickory slab. They lasted twenty or thirty years. Then he and some of the neighbors employed a ditching machine. It consisted of a heavy angle iron at the end of which was a seven-inch ball with a nose. It was dragged upright through the soil by capistan and oxen, the ball making the underground ditch from pond to outlet. There was a level to determine the depth. Some of the "mole" ditches worked well for twenty-five years, in clay soil even longer. Mr. Oakwood later was the first to use tile in this section. Now there are no swamps and no standing ponds except where deepened artificially.

His son Thomas has the yoke that the oxen wore when breaking much virgin prairie soil and the last in this neighborhood. He himself, when a lad of fifteen in 1813 drove the oxen with it on to hand feed for seventy-five head of cattle. He says it is in perfect condition and he will loan it to anyone who needs it.

The improvement in farm machinery has been steady and great, from the walking plow, to the riding plow and the tractor, from the cradle to reaper to self-binder. In 1884 Levi Vinson had the first self-binder, a

McCormick, in his neighborhood, northwest of Oakwood. It used wire for bands. Lem Collett had the first in the Oakwood neighborhood in the late seventies. It also used wire: John Clapp and his son Daniel bought the first one to use twine a few years later. It was the Excelsior.

A combine that threshes as it cuts is now used by a few. The latest is the one picker which has at last proved a success. Fred Dalbey has used a one-row picker for several years. This year two, Glenn Ilk and Richard Green each can pick a load in about half an hour. They cost $575.

The price of land steadily increased. In 1880 the Will Oakwood farm northeast of town was bought for $14 per acre. When John Davidson soon after bought better drained land near it at $50, may shook their heads and said John could never pay for it. He sold it in 1919 for $225. Lincoln H. Green and W.G. Green bought 240 acres of the old Colby farm northwest of Bronson in 1891 at $52.50 per acre. By 1898 a few pieces sold for $100. During the Great War the price was boomed to $250 or $300, and corn bought $2 per bushel. For some of the highly improved land much more was offered. Then came the deflation and scarcely half of that price could be obtained now. But not much land is selling. Farmers have been particularly hard hit by the period of readjustment. In spite of the crop short from drought, corn is but $.61 December first, wheat $.64.

Mills were of course needed as soon as the grain was rippened. The "corn-cracker" was first and very crude. It consisted of a four-foot section of a hollow log two feet in diameter into which a flat stone was fitted. A handle was fitted into a hole drilled into a "nigger head," a small granite boulder, and it was rocked and pushed with a rotary motion on the flat stone. A strong man could crack about a bushel of corn an hour. In 1826 an old water grist mill was in active operation on Salt Fork. People came as far as from McLean County to have grinding done. About 1832 or 1833 a grist mill on Middle Fork had also a saw mill added. Soon there were other mills. Now in 1930, there are no water mills, no grist mills, but here and there small iron and steel private mills run by tractors. The same is true of saw mills.

Modern transportation has altered many things. There was a tile mill in the east side of Oakwood in 1884 run by James Rector and William

Johnson. Nettie Redman's twin brother was killed on the belt when he was a boy, working for spending money. The mill ran about six years. A few bricks were made. The pit about three feet deep, from which the clay had been taken, soon filled with water and was known as Longstreth's pond. He deepened it and cut ice from it. It was a much enjoyed skating rink in winter and also playground in summer. It is told that some of our leading citizens got their first experience of the evils of using tobacco while playing hooky on its banks. It is now drained and nearly filled up. In 1918 when it was about to go dry, they called Roy Green to save the fish, catfish and put them in his deeper pond.

Coal mining has been a major industry. Mr. Vance is the first known to have used coal as fuel. In 1830, just 100 years ago, he used it in the furnace under his salt kettles.

It is said that one early settler on the north road to Danville near "Hungry Hollow" finding some smooth black rocks, built himself a nice fireplace in his cabin. It drew well. To his amazement, not only the wood, but the fireplace itself was consumed!

When the coal banks were first opened southeast of Oakwood, anyone could have all he wanted for nothing if he would dig it himself. The first to mine and haul coal to sell was Rice and Co. This was before the railroad. They hauled it with teams to Champaign and other counties. After the railroad came, the coal mining industry was rapidly extended.

In 1873 William and Henry Butler contracted with the Consolidated Coal Company to strip the earth from the coal in Missionfield. Huge dredge boats were set up and the earth turned in great ridges. Now, having been abandoned years ago when the coal was all taken, it looks as though ancient giants had plowed the pleasant valley and sown destruction. The barren or overgrown ridges alternate with ditches of stagnant water, dangerously deep in placc. In these ditches are fish and many frogs. They have been nicknamed "The Polliwogs" for years. Now nearly all the coal has been removed from the Salt Fork valley to the mouth of the Middle Fork.

One of the largest dredge boats in the world is operating along the Middle Fork. Glenburn, a few miles north of Oakwood, had shaft mines and was at one time a thriving village. The mines were closed about 1900 and nearly all the houses sold and moved away. When Mr. Fern became operator here in 1918, four large mining companies were shipping many carloads of coal from this point. Now but one, and it does not work steadily. Sometime the better coal in the deeper veins will be needed. The raising of the cattle and hogs was once a more extensive business than at present. Mont Fox, Dick Seymour and others are fattening sheep brought from the west. Poultry has always been an adjunct of farming. Mrs. Anna Oakwood remembers when there was no market here for hens and how irritated they were to sell a few for $1.50 a dozen. When they left the farm near Fithian about 1880, they sold 100 chickens and young for $10. Eggs were three dozen for a quarter or less and butter 15 or 18 cents. Today, December 3, 1930, the Danville paper quotes hens at 15 cents and eggs 35 cents per dozen, both considered low for this season of the year, butterfat, 42 cents. Many raise broilers from chicks from the commercial hatcheries for the early markets. Many farmers' wives also purchase their early baby chicks.

James Carpenter has been drilling wells for seventeen years. His well-drilling machine and equipment is doubtless the best in this part of the state and he can furnish supplies for all sorts of wells. He has drilled hundreds of wells from 4-inches to 18-inches in diameter and can go 500 feet down. He has sounded for railroad bridge abutments and has prospected for geologists. He can tell interesting things about the earth's strata. About 1914 progressive citizens financed a drilling for oil at Glenburn without success. Small amounts of gas and oil may be found, however, when drilling for water in other places near.

A creamery company was organized in 1908 and a building built on the corner of Wed Hillman's farm just east of town. Many citizens bought shares. It made good butter, but ran only three or four years for there was not enough cream to make it profitable.

Schools

The first school building in the township was built in 1829 near the present site of Newtown. The next is thought to have been the Merry Posy School on the north side of the State Road not far from the present Lakeshore School. No date fan be found, but about 1840 when Michael Oakwood, who presumably attended there had learned his "three R's—Reading, 'riting, and 'rithmatic" and wanted to study grammar, his teacher had studied it, but had no book. The book venders in Danville had none, nor had they ever had a call for it, for grammar was not studied in Vermillion County. They told him he might borrow one from some cultured family from the east, which he did, until a neighbor driving cattle to Chicago brought back the coveted book.

Mr. Clapp also remembers attending school in Finley Chapel while the school house at Blue Corners was being built. The second school house, or third, was built there before it the school was moved to Oakwood in 1892.

Mr. John C. Randall, principal and Myrtle Young assistant were teaching eighty-three youngsters in all grades from six to twenty years of age in the one-room of the old building, two classes on the floor at the same time. "It was sure some job," says Mr. Randall, and we can believe it. The summer term began on April 1 and about May 1 the upper room of the new two-room building in Oakwood was near enough completion on the lot where Smith Mason now lives to permit Mr. Randall to move in with about thirty pupils. He mentions their happy times together which he often recalls.

He gives the following names of some of the pupils: Sammie Longstrech; Eddie Snyder, George Hillman, Joseph Redman, Thomas Harrison, Scott Harrison, Edward Reeves, John Reeves, Thomas Sailor, Charlotte Blake, Artie Van Atta, Ida Smith, Maggie Blake, Rachel Blake, Nettie Redman, Carric Burgess, Stella Oakwood, Laura Dalbey, Chris Dalbey, Charles Wainwright, Jake Devors, Litill Smith, J. Truax, Fannie Doggett. The directors were Dr. J. Laelin, Amos Seymour, and L.G. Colett.

In the fall of 1892, Otis B. Haworth became Principal. He graded the school and with the cooperation of the directors organized a two-year high school. On June 1, 1894, S.B. Longstrech was the first and only graduate. For graduation exercises the seniors gave a play, *The Irish Linen Peddler*.

The principal taught the seventh and eighth grades and the high school subjects. J.H. Elliott and George Weizer were outstanding principals of the three-year high school. Later two more rooms were added making possible another year of high school. In 1914 the present high was erected a block south on the east side of the street. Victor Gorman was principal.

After the township high school was built, the high school course was discontinued. The four rooms are not occupied by 101 pupils in the grades. Mr. Charles Huddleson, the principal, is teaching the fifth and sixth grades. Miss Lucile Liggett taught primary for three years and Eva Diggs new this year in the lower grades. Mr. Haworth was principal of Oakwood for some time, the elected County Superintendent, which office he filled for twelve years. He was a great help when the Oakwood Township High School was organized. It has a beautiful building in a beautiful location near Stoney Creek on the old State Road. The first school was held in it in 1916-1917. Mr. Glenn Smith was principal of the school.

Dr. Michaels of Muncie has been president of the school board since its beginning. He was also elected this year president of the Vermillion County Medical Association. E.K. Congran is the present principal, and seven others are teaching all the courses in an up-to-date high school. The enrollment is about 150. There were 24 graduates this spring. The Building bonds are being retired. The board this year was able to buy two busses and hire on other to accommodate the students, which aids attendance.

However, it must be noted that one celebrated her one-hundredth birthday last February—Mrs. Elizabeth Neal, wife of our veteran blacksmith, Brad Neal. He is the oldest man in active business, longer in the same business at the same place than any other—thirty-seven years.

Any interesting anecdotes must also be omitted, such as the time the Indians so frightened the women of the first Henry Oakwood family by coming to the door whetting huge butcher knives in their hands. Though they were smiling, the women thought they were threatening until they understood a whetstone was desired.

The darkness and mud of the streets is recalled when J. Smith Mason tells how, on alighting from the train when they arrived here from Ohio in 1881, his hat blew off and they had to borrow a lantern and wade to find it.

To recapitulate, Oakwood's in a location of historical interest in the county and state, has also within a few minutes' drive, bluffs and deposits, fossils, flowers and ferns and trees, which make it a favorite study ground of the Natural History Department of our great University. Its scenery attracts the camera hunter and camper.

Oakwood though surrounded by abundant soil for the farmer, yet is within easy reach abundance of coal for fuel and timber for rough construction. It has good drainage. It is near enough to Danville, the county seat, that many find employment there as well as a good market and shopping place.

Oakwood, a place of pleasant streets and happy homes—may she never be less!

Authors: ClassThree
(Oakwood Methodist Church Sunday School)

Helen Oakwood
Margaret Davis
Dorothy Seymour
Meridith Crawford
Billy Snider
Junior Frances
Norma Snider
Mary C. Green, Historian (researcher)
Mary E. Meade, Typist

About the Author

Katherine R. "Kit" Inman was born in St. Louis, raised across the Mississippi in Illinois, received her AB and BS from the University of Illinois and her MA from the State University of Iowa in Creative Writing. After teaching high school for three years, she married her college sweetheart, Capt. Lloyd J. Inman. A "war bride," she worked as a claim adjuster during WWII. After returning from the war, her husband decided to join the regular army, so she focused on being an Army wife and Mother of three sons, occasionally teaching after her sons were in school.

With her sons grown, she taught English in college for seven years, and after retirement, still loving teaching, she taught advanced Bible Studies for thirty years, and oil painting for about ten years—simultaneously. She has been writing since she was six years old, 731 poems, 7 books, 23 short stories, one novel, and innumerable short recorded thoughts. She has been painting for years, and is planning a set of miniatures, one for each of the 50 states.

Kit loves people, loves the Lord, and enjoys all kinds of things. Her grandmother, Mary C. Green, was her mentor and inspiration—along with her parents Alta and Wilfred Ropiequet. Her writings reflect her positive attitude, faith, and love of life. Now 91, she appreciates all the help of family and friends, but she's still active and excited about life.

Many of her writings are posted on her website, www.kit-inman.com More will come as her son finds time to add them.

A recent photo of author Katherine R. "Kit" Inman.

Other Books by Katherine R. Inman

His Best - Life of Lloyd J. Inman

Free Land